D1595683

GORDON TULLOCK is Professor of Economics and
Public Choice at Virginia Polytechnic Institute.
Generally regarded as one of the founders of the
"new political economy," Professor Tullock is the
author of, among many other works, **The Politics
of Bureaucracy** (1965), **The Organization of Inquiry**
(1965), and with James M. Buchanan, **The Calculus
of Consent** (1962).

# PRIVATE WANTS,
# PUBLIC MEANS

# PRIVATE
# WANTS,
# PUBLIC
# MEANS

An Economic Analysis
of the Desirable Scope
of Government

## GORDON TULLOCK

BASIC BOOKS, INC.

*Publishers*

NEW YORK                    LONDON

# Preface

The conventional wisdom holds that the market is made up of private persons trying to benefit themselves, but that the government is concerned with something called the public interest. In recent years this approach has been challenged by a new theory of government. This theory, originally developed by such economists as Pigou and Samuelson, has provided a foundation for what can only be described as an economic theory of politics. The purpose of this book is not to elaborate this new theory of politics but to apply it to the particular problem of what the state should do. The main analytical tool to be used will be the economics of externalities.

In general, if we see someone doing something, we believe that it is something that he wants to do and will improve his well-being. Similarly, if we see several people agreeing to do something or to make exchanges among themselves, we normally assume that they will all benefit —again, because their acts are all voluntary. It is our usual belief that human beings only voluntarily do things that they want to do. The vast superstructure of economics has been built upon the analysis of such voluntary acts. If, however, we observe individual acts or voluntary agreements, we will frequently find that someone other than the acting individual or the people who are participating in the agreement is affected by that act or agreement. Where this is so, we have an externality. Since the publication of Samuelson's basic work in the early 1950's, most economists have justified the existence of government as a device to deal with these externalities. This justification will be one of the two main themes of this book.

Government action, however, requires some kind of decision process. Such decision processes are extremely varying; in one case, it may simply be "do what Mao says"; on the other hand, as in a legal case, it may be decided by a random sample of twelve individuals voting unanimously. Whatever the decision process is, however, it necessarily disadvantages at least somebody. Thus, if private acts may create externalities on other persons, then governmental acts also disadvantage certain individuals. This injury to at least some members of the community from acts of government is the second main theme of this book. The injuries that externalities may inflict on individuals if everything is left to the market and the injuries that government may inflict on individuals through the inherent nature of its decision process are the two basic factors in selecting the proper institutions to deal with any given problem. We must always weigh the specific advantages and disadvantages of these two imperfect instrumentalities.

The purpose of this book, then, is not very revolutionary. Everything that I have said thus far will seem quite conventional to the modern welfare economist. Nevertheless, I believe that there has not yet been any general effort to systematically develop the implications of these two principles in dealing with the scope of government. My intent is to fill this gap. Professional welfare economists may well find it prosaic and unimaginative. Conventional political scientists, on the other hand, are rather apt to regard the book as perverse. It makes almost no use of their traditional tools.

The plan of the book is simple. After a first chapter in which the tools are illustrated with an example, we have a rather long theoretical development of these two techniques. We then proceed to a large number of concrete applications in Part II and a brief conclusion in the final chapter.

The actual genesis of this book was not in the mind of the author but in that of Arthur Seldon of the Institute of Economic Affairs. My debt of gratitude to Seldon is magnified by the fact that he showed my first draft to Edward Mishan. Mishan's detailed notes were a great help in improving the manuscript. I am particularly grateful to Mishan, since it is clear that on a number of matters, he and I have rather different approaches. A critic of high technical competence, but with philosophical differences with the author, is ideal. Many of Mishan's comments have been incorporated into the final draft, although some differences of attitude and approach have remained. As is normal with my books, James Buchanan read the manuscript and made a number of helpful suggestions. I should also like to thank the students in my class in Economics 417 who had the book, in a rather badly reproduced version, inflicted on them as a text. Not only did they catch me in two minor but potentially embarrassing technical errors but their comments were a great help in improving the expository qualities of the manuscript. The title for this book was suggested by my colleague, Charles Goetz. It seems to me that it is not only a good book title but very neatly summarizes the new method of thinking about government.

GORDON TULLOCK

CENTER FOR STUDY OF PUBLIC CHOICE
VIRGINIA POLYTECHNIC INSTITUTE

*Blacksburg, Virginia*
*June 1970*

# Contents

# PART

# I

# THEORY

# Mosquito Abatement

In Illinois where I was born, and indeed in most of the two American continents, the common mosquito is a major pest.[1] The American Indians adapted to this pest by developing immunity, and the early settlers, by swearing. In the nineteenth century and the early twentieth century, however, a method of protecting oneself from the mosquito when indoors was developed: the window and door screen. With the discovery that the mosquito was not only a pest but a carrier of a number of fairly nasty diseases, more radical methods of control were adopted in some areas. The construction of the Panama Canal vitally depended upon an extensive program for limiting the number of malaria-carrying mosquitoes and keeping the workers on the canal within screened areas so that they were unlikely to be bitten by even the few mosquitoes that remained. In the more temperate zones of the United States, malaria and

[1] Actually the common mosquito is a popular name, not a biological name. Quite a number of species of the same general type of insect are involved.

3

yellow fever were a less serious menace, but the mosquito was still a nuisance. As a result, in a number of communities, notably Chicago, programs were instituted in the 1920's and 1930's to reduce the number of mosquitoes by attacks on their breeding areas. These programs in general were modeled on those that had been developed in Panama, but were not as extensive. The reduction in the number of mosquitoes from these programs was relatively small but meaningful.

With the development of DDT during World War II, a much cheaper way of reducing the mosquito population became available, and many communities hired aircraft in the years after World War II to spray areas with DDT. Recently this spraying has become much less common, partially as a result of a realization that DDT has other effects on the natural environment than the reduction of the mosquitoes and that some of these other effects may be quite undesirable, and partially as a result of the adoption of home air-conditioning. A person living in an air-conditioned house is unlikely to spend anywhere near as much time exposed to mosquitoes in the summer as a person living in a non-air-conditioned house. As a consequence, the amount of aerial spraying of DDT has been reduced considerably in recent years, and a number of other techniques that are both less effective in dealing with mosquitoes and more expensive have been adopted, but on a smaller scale.

The reader may wonder why a book on government should begin with a technological discussion of a minor local problem. The reason is simple. Almost all of the problems involved in decisions as to what activities should be undertaken by the government are found in this simple example. Furthermore, there is nothing in the way of a traditional solution to this problem. One of the great problems in talking about the new discoveries in the field of social cost, externalities, and the economics of the government sector is that most people have been thoroughly indoctrinated with the existing tradition. Those who have not learned the orthodox tradition normally learn some particularly strong attack on it, which is in many ways just another tradition. Thus a discussion of government activities runs into a barrier of strongly held ideas. If we discuss mosquito abatement, however, we normally find a complete absence of these traditions or antitraditions and hence we can deal with the problem with less emotional difficulty. Since recent developments in economics make it possible to rethink almost all of our basic ideas in this field and place them on a sounder basis, our avoidance of "conditioned reactions" is vital.[2] The first steps in this rethinking will be outlined in this book. I must confess, however, that much of the material in the book will not be original. Still, what I have to say will seem new, and perhaps strange, to that 99.99 per cent of the population who have not been keeping up with recent developments in the rather arcane fields of welfare economics and public finance. Thus, the use of an example that is free from emotional and traditional overtones seems desirable.

To return, then, to the mosquitoes, let us assume that we are in 1952 (and, as we will discover reading through this book, the specific technology in any given time is a highly important matter in deciding whether a given activity should be handled by the government, by private enter-

[2] It does not follow from the fact that we rethink them that the conclusions we reach will be radically different from the tradition. The rethinking in fact will indicate that a good portion of the tradition is correct.

prise, by the central government, by the local government, or perhaps should be simply left completely untouched) and that we are living in a small town in Iowa where the mosquito problem is serious. Presumably we already have screens on our houses. However, since we go outdoors fairly frequently in the summer, mosquitoes are a serious problem to us. There are several ways for us to deal with the problem of mosquitoes. First, of course, we could reduce the amount of time we spend outdoors, and everyone who lives in an area where mosquitoes are prevalent does indeed do this. Second, there were as of 1952 certain creams and greases that could be placed on exposed skin areas to repel mosquitoes. Unfortunately, these preparations also tended to keep people away because they gave off a peculiar odor. Nevertheless, for anyone who had to go into the woods or along a stream, the use of these creams was a sensible precaution. Third, we could undertake a spraying campaign in our own backyard. We could buy a suitable insect spray in a local supermarket and spray our backyard and perhaps spray a little into our neighbor's yard. This spray would generally reduce the number of mosquitoes in the area, partly by killing the ones that were there at the time of the spraying and partly because a residuum of the spray was left on the vegetation, and mosquitoes landing on the residuum might be killed. Nevertheless, the last method would be an expensive and inefficient way of reducing the number of mosquitoes in an immediate vicinity. It was used, however, particularly by people who were planning garden parties.

Another method of mosquito abatement was available, however. For a small sum of approximately fifty dollars, an airplane could be chartered to spray an entire town with DDT, which would produce considerable mosquito abate-

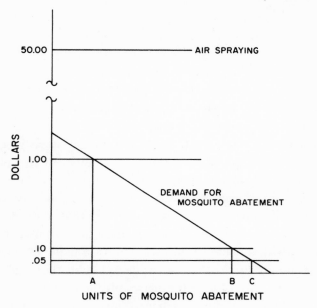

FIGURE 1. Individual Choice of Mosquito Abatement

ment. More frequent spraying would lead to more deaths of mosquitoes. The situation is illustrated in Figure 1. For an individual, the demand for mosquito abatement is shown by the slanting line. If he chooses the hand spray method, then the line marked one dollar will indicate the cost of killing one unit of mosquitoes in his yard. The individual will choose to purchase A units, and his total cost is represented by the rectangle to the left of A. The individual would not be interested in hiring an airplane because he can obtain any amount of mosquito abatement in his own yard more cheaply by hand spraying than by spraying from the air.

The situation changes radically, however, if the individual joins together with the other citizens of the town to hire the airplane. If there are 1,000 citizens in the town, the cost to each one for mosquito abatement in his backyard falls to five cents a unit and the total amount consumed would rise to C. Under these circumstances, the entire mosquito abatement demand would be met by air spraying rather than hand spraying because, once again, this particular technological method is strictly dominant.[3]

Clearly, at these prices, if the individual were given a choice he would prefer C mosquito abatement by air spraying to A units produced by hand spraying. Thus one could present a good argument for the collective provision of mosquito abatement. Suppose, however, that instead of a government agency undertaking mosquito abatement, a private effort is made to induce various individuals to contribute money to charter the airplane. Under these circumstances, the cost of chartering an airplane depends upon the number of people who have contributed. If only 500 people are willing to contribute, then the cost of the mosquito abatement by air (per unit) is ten cents and they would then choose to purchase the amount B.

Assuming that this voluntary method of mosquito abatement is adopted, the individual would be sensible not to make the payment. If he is not a member of the group making the payment, he receives the mosquito abatement free. If, on the other hand, he decides to make his payment, and we assume that the amount of money he puts in is then invested in purchasing additional aircraft time for the whole city, he then faces a purchase price for mosquito abatement in his yard of fifty dollars a unit. This price is

[3] In actual practice, the demand may be for spraying at certain times, and an individual who is having a garden party several days after the last spraying may also engage in hand spraying. We need not bother with this complication.

clearly far above the amount that he wishes to pay. The general discussion of the bargaining problems that would arise if we attempted to handle problems of this sort through voluntary provision will be deferred until a later chapter. It is unlikely, however, that individuals would be willing to made a voluntary contribution. Normally only a government could provide the airplane spraying.[4]

Of course, the possibility always exists that some individual may believe that he is influential enough so that everyone else will copy his action. If this individual feels this way he would logically become a member of the group that plans to charter the airplane. Clearly, however, not everybody can entertain such delusions of grandeur. Hence, if voluntary renting of the airplane were suggested, the bulk of the community would be unwilling to make payments. We thus have what appears to be a fairly unambiguous argument for a governmental agency compelling the citizens of this small town to pay for the chartering of an airplane. The citizens themselves would be better off under this arrangement and would presumably favor it.

It has been, however, an implicit assumption in the discussion so far that each citizen has exactly the same demand for mosquito abatement. Presumably, this is not true and indicates that a decision must be made as to how much mosquito abatement should be purchased. In order to consider this decision, let us now examine Figure 2 in which the demand curves for mosquito abatement of three citizens (Mr. A, Mr. B, and Mr. C) are shown. Note that if there is no decision to charter an airplane, the three individuals

---

[4] Sometimes informal pressures can function very much like a government. As a general rule, however, human experience seems to indicate that informal pressure is not sufficient and we normally use governmental coercion in such cases.

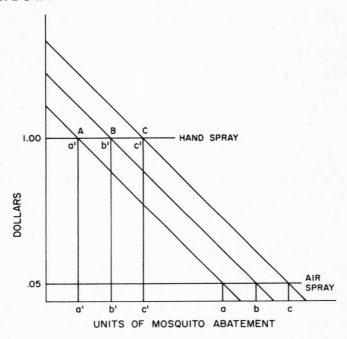

FIGURE 2. Mosquito Abatement with Majority Vote

will simply purchase different numbers of units of mosquito abatement through the use of the hand spray: Mr. A purchasing a' units, Mr. B purchasing b' units, and Mr. C purchasing c' units.

If, however, the citizens decide to rent an airplane and engage in collective provision of mosquito abatement, then a decision must be made as to how much mosquito abatement should be purchased. The three individuals have three different ideas regarding the amount of abatement—represented by a, b, and c on the diagram. This example is carefully constructed so that their preferences on this par-

ticular point would be what is known as "single peaked."[5]
If we consider ourselves as dealing with only a three-man
community that makes decisions by a majority vote (and
this particular type of situation presents arguments for doing this), then we would predict that the three men would
purchase the amount b of mosquito abatement. Thus, Mr.
A and Mr. C have failed to obtain their optimum amount
of mosquito abatement.

It does not follow, of course, from the fact that the individuals could make a perfect adjustment of how much
mosquito abatement they wish to purchase if they use hand
spray. In most cases they must anticipate that they will not
get their first choice of quantity if the government provides the spraying, and that hand spraying is superior. It
merely follows that in collective action a cost is involved
that should be considered. Assuming again that we have our
society of 1,000 people, I would compare my likely purchase of spray with what I thought was the likely outcome
of the voting process in terms of the amount that would be
obtained by collective provision. I would anticipate that the
amount provided collectively would not turn out to be
exactly the amount that I wanted. I presume that in areas
where mosquitoes are prevalent most people would choose
the collective provision. Note, however, that this means
that they are choosing a less than optimal arrangement of
the resource by their own preference ordering. In a sense,
an externality is imposed upon them by the choice of the
collective decision process; they will no longer be able to
make an ideal adjustment.

We have, however, imposed a further unrealistic as-

[5] Cf. Duncan Black, *The Theory of Committees and Elections* (Cambridge: Cambridge University Press, 1958).

sumption by assuming that the only way of obtaining collective mosquito abatement is through airplane spraying. This method, in fact, is not even common today and never was the only one used, although at one time it was widely thought to be the cheapest. If we include the possibility of mosquito abatement by other methods, then the simple single-peaked structure that we put into this system disappears and the end product is likely to be more complicated. It is also likely that the individual will find the outcome further from his own optima and therefore the use of collective decision techniques involves a greater cost to the individual. It still, of course, does not follow that collective decision-making is inferior to private decision-making, and, once again, I presume that most people who live in areas where mosquitoes are prevalent would prefer collective mosquito abatement. I am not arguing against collective decision-making, but am simply pointing out that like market decision-making, it also has a cost. In each case we must weigh the cost against the benefit, and in the particular case we are now discussing, I think we would all agree that the benefit is greater than the cost.

It should be noted, however, that for some people in the community, the cost of this type of collective mosquito abatement was great. Let us suppose that a genuine American Indian with his inherited immunity to mosquito bites lives in the community. Presumably he would not voluntarily purchase mosquito abatement and would regard the necessity of paying taxes to purchase mosquito abatement under collective decision-making as an unmitigated wrong. In his case the choice of the collective decision-making process rather than private decision-making process is clearly undesirable. As a general rule, people whose personal preferences are markedly unconventional or markedly different from those of the community are likely to be injured by collective decision-making procedures. Fortunately, for most people concerning most issues, our preferences are not so radically different from the norm as to cause collective decision-making to be necessarily inferior.

As another example, we may assume that at the time we conducted our mental experiment, one member of the community had read Rachel Carson's *The Silent Spring*. He would regard the aerial spraying of the town as positively dangerous, a creator of illth. Thus he would be opposed to it and would obtain considerable dissatisfaction from the spraying even if he did not have to pay for it himself. He may, however, be strongly in favor of mosquito abatement by other methods. Once again, we are faced with someone who would object strenuously to the use of collective methods. The costs of collective as against private provision characteristically depend upon two things: the preference of the people making the decisions and the available technology. Frequently, for people with unusual preferences, costs of public provision of facilities are extremely great. If everybody has similar preferences, technology may make collective provision inefficient. The working out of the details of these relationships will fill many chapters in the latter part of this book.

The reader may well be interested in whether simple majority voting is the most efficient way of achieving a decision as to the amount of air spraying to be used in a particular case. This is an interesting and important question, but will not be discussed greatly in this book. The reason is not that I object to talking about it but that I have already talked about it a great deal in other books and probably will continue to talk about it in still further books.[6] For the time being we can simply say that if we assume that individuals have relatively similar preference intensities or that preference intensities are randomly distributed, then the single-peak preference curve and simple majority voting lead to what can reasonably be described as a "good" outcome. If we do not make these assumptions, more complicated arrangements are desirable. This book will not discuss these more complicated arrangements.

We can, however, say *something* about desirable political arrangements for our mosquito abatement program. As a beginning, we may inquire as to what is the ideal size of the government unit to deal with this program. First, we should note the limits that are placed upon this method by the technology of aircraft spraying. In order to be efficient in abating mosquitoes over our small town, the aircraft should spray the entire town and certain nearby mosquito breeding areas. An effort to spray half of the town would give much less than half the protection; it would be a bad bargain. Therefore, the minimum size of a government unit that decides to hire the airplane should be our small town in the Middle West.

We may, however, inquire whether this size is also the optimum. For this purpose, let us turn to Figure 3. On the horizontal axis of Figure 3, we have once again drawn in the units of mosquito abatement. Then on the vertical axis we have shown the number of people who have as their optimum any particular amount of mosquito abatement. Our method is a type of short-hand compression of one of

[6] Gordon Tullock, *The Calculus of Consent*, with James M. Buchanan (Ann Arbor: University of Michigan Press, 1962), and *Toward A Mathematics of Politics* (Ann Arbor: University of Michigan Press, 1966).

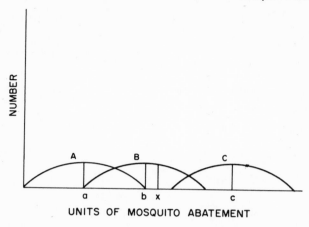

UNITS OF MOSQUITO ABATEMENT

FIGURE 3. Distribution of Preferences on Mosquito Abatement

Duncan Black's sets of single-peak preference curves. We have drawn in the optima collections for three different communities (A, B, and C). It will be noted that each of these has a somewhat different distribution of optima, which could result from different technological conditions —for example, community C may be located close to a swamp—or to simple differences in taste.

In any event, we would anticipate that different communities would not have identical preferences. For any individual community it can be demonstrated that the midpoint in the preference distribution is the "policy" that comes closest to optimizing the preferences of the entire community under our assumptions. Thus, the individual communities could select the amounts of spraying shown by a, b, and c. If the communities join together and all vote on a standard amount of spraying, however, they would end up at point x. For all three communities, this would be less satisfactory than the optima for their individual community, although it would be the best policy

15

to be followed assuming we must choose a uniform policy for the three communities.[7] Thus, a substantial loss is involved in combining the three communities into one for purposes of making decisions on mosquito abatement. The optimal size of the collective unit for this decision would be the individual community.

In part, this conclusion is a result of the available technology. It is possible that a large metropolis (such as Chicago) would find that the technologically optimal area would be small enough so that subsections of the metropolis could efficiently vote themselves on the amount of spraying. This problem necessarily involves detailed technological investigations.

Rather than having all of the communities joining together to vote on a single level of spraying for all of them, they could form a large group of communities that would then select different amounts of spraying for each individual community. If this large unit determined the amount of spraying for each individual unit by conducting a local plebiscite, there would be no objection to this procedure but also no obvious reason for the existence of the large unit. If, on the other hand, the entire unit voted on a complex plan involving different levels of spraying in different communities, one would anticipate that the outcome may be highly nonoptimal. First, there is no obvious reason why the citizens of community C should be well informed about the needs of community A. Insofar as their votes have any effect on the amount of spraying that will be undertaken in community A, at best, this is the addition of ran-

---

[7] For a general proof see Yoram Barzel, "Two Propositions on the Optimal Level of Producing Collective Goods," *Public Choice* 6 (Spring 1969): 31-37.

dom noise to the decision process and generally tends to lower its efficiency.

More important, however, there is no strong reason to believe that the communities will have a totally altruistic approach to these problems. Surely a proposal under which communities A and B tax community C for the purpose of spraying themselves would be a continuing danger. If we look at real-world politics, we can observe that this type of situation is quite common. It does not take the form of straightforward exploitation of one community in all cases, although such examples can be found. More normally, it takes the form of logrolling in which all communities receive some spraying, and, in fact, the general level of spraying granted the assumptions we have made, would be way above the optima that the individual communities would select for themselves.[8] This again would be a substantial inefficiency. Thus, it would appear that the lowest cost method is to let the communities determine how much spraying they want for themselves. In other words, the optimal collective unit is the small city.

We can, however, turn to another matter here. It may seem tedious for each small community to vote yearly on mosquito abatement. It is not clear why we feel this way. We are never particularly concerned about the possibility that individuals will spend too much time making private decisions. If private mosquito abatement were used in these communities, each individual would have decided for himself whether he needed a new can of spray and whether to go out in the yard and spray. It is not exactly obvious why we should be disturbed by the prospect that he would have

[8] Cf. Gordon Tullock, "Problems of Majority Voting," *Journal of Political Economy*, 67, no. 6 (June 1956): 571–579.

somewhat the same amount of decision-making time involved in deciding whether or not the city should have an airplane for the same purpose.

It may be that the reason we attempt to economize on decision-making efforts for collective decisions and not on private decisions is simply that our present mechanisms for making collective decisions are complex and inconvenient. Going to the polls to cast a vote on an issue is in many ways an expensive process. If this is the only reason we worry, then technology is rapidly coming to our rescue. In a few years it will be quite possible for everyone to attach a device to his telephone that permits him to express his opinions on any issue. If the only reason we attempt to economize on the time spent in voting is that present-day methods of voting are quite inconvenient, this matter will shortly be a matter of past history.[9]

Still, under present circumstances, we do attempt to economize on the number of votes in individual communities. Our usual method is to have the votes cast on a collection of issues at a single time rather than on a single issue. For example, we may vote on an individual or a board to make decisions for the small community. In this case, the voting decisions are made on a complex of different matters. First, the candidates presumably will have made statements as to what they propose to do and we can choose the one that seems most desirable to us; second, we will be interested in the personality of the individuals concerned. In the real world this personal interest is apt to be rather wide. Whether Mrs. Jones or Mrs. Smith is the more attractive woman may have considerable influence on whether Mr. Jones or Mr. Smith is elected. In any event, if we cast our

---

[9] Cf. James C. Miller, III, "A Program for Direct and Proxy Voting in the Legislative Process," *Public Choice*, 7 (Fall 1969): 107–113.

votes in such a way that each vote affects a number of issues, some of which concern the personalities of the candidates, we can anticipate that we will have considerably
poorer adjustment in the decision on mosquito spraying
than if we had a specific vote on that particular issue.

This is so for several reasons; first, there is the noise
effect. I can communicate less information to the "government" by a single vote covering eight or nine issues than
by eight or nine separate votes. I should anticipate, therefore, that the government will be less closely attuned to my
desires. To some extent this is offset by the possibility of
logrolling if the vote is made on a collection of issues. The
individual candidates make up a "platform" appealing to
different people, which permits them to take into account
the intensity of individual preferences. Thus, I may find
myself selecting a candidate whose views on the amount of
mosquito spraying are quite radically different from my
own because I like his views on other matters. My voting
for this candidate will reduce my degree of satisfaction
from mosquito spraying, although it may improve my degree of satisfaction with the activities of the town government as a whole.

The second reason one may anticipate poorer adjustment in the amount of mosquito spraying if mosquito
spraying is voted on together with a number of other issues
is, simply, that it is a harder choice to make. I cannot think
of the matter in relatively simple terms, but must consider
it in terms of interrelation with a number of different issues.
Since the matter is not very important, I may be well ad-
vised not to think much about it and to accept a poor
decision as opposed to using much energy in an attempt
to reach a good decision.

Some *bona fide* political theories argue that we should

leave decisions on such matters to a government servant. Theoreticians differ as to whether the servant is to be elected, selected by examination, or appointed by a divine king. What we should note here is that if we are simply leaving the decision to someone who is selected on other characteristics, then we are accepting a fairly large random variable in the decision on mosquito abatement. Under these circumstances we would anticipate that the amount of mosquito spraying would be more deviant from that of the individual than if the decision were made by simple majority voting.

It does not follow from these costs incurred by deviating from a simple majority vote on the amount of mosquito spraying that we should not so deviate. The reduction in cost that can come from reducing the number of votes that individuals must undertake is a real one, and it should be balanced against the additional cost imposed by other methods of making decisions. Here we have what amounts to an empirical problem, and a problem that has not yet been subject to any substantial empirical research. It does, however, appear to be a researchable problem, and we can hope that such research will give us a better idea of how many issues we should vote on directly and how many we should deal with in clusters.

So far, we have been discussing the problem of mosquito abatement as it existed about ten years ago. Since that time considerable technological change has taken place. Let us confine ourselves to considering only those technological changes that have indicated that the simple airplane spraying of DDT is not desirable. It has been realized that a large number of secondary costs result from this operation and that these secondary costs may well be much in excess of the benefits derived. As a result, the technology of mosquito abatement now no longer depends mainly on this extremely cheap method. We need not go into the more complicated and more expensive methods that are now in general use; it is perfectly possible that tomorrow someone will invent another, and better, method. We can simply note that present methods are expensive and inquire what effect this would have on our decision.

The first possible effect of the increase in the expense of mosquito abatement by collective measures may be that the unit cost of a given amount of mosquito abatement would be equal or higher if one uses the collective methods than if one restricts mosquito abatement to the private use of sprays in one's own backyard. In this easy case, the proper decision, of course, would be to completely abandon all collective efforts to reduce mosquitoes and let individuals make their own decisions.[10] The second possibility (also very easy) is that mosquito abatement either by public or by private means may become so expensive that it would no longer be desired. Once again, the proper solution is to have no public program, and we would anticipate that there

---

[10] Conceivably, it may be possible to purchase the mosquito spraying devices for the individual household more economically if the city bought them than if the individual did. Under these circumstances, collective provision of the individual sprays could (if the saving in money was large enough) be justified on exactly the same reasoning as airplane spraying. It would also be at least theoretically possible for the community to purchase the mosquito spray and then distribute it to the households, even if there was no economy involved. This would have the disadvantage that if every household were given the same amount, it would mean that most households were not in appropriate adjustment. Any effort on the part of the government to guess the demands for mosquito abatement of the individual citizens and provide them with a number of bug bombs and presumably a tax bill proportionate to their demand would most assuredly be abortive.

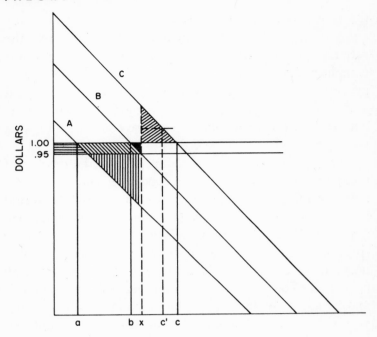

FIGURE 4. Costs and Benefits of Collectivization

would be no private abatement either. Both of these are easy problems and in both cases we need go no further with our analysis.

The interesting question, however, is what we would do if the use of various public means for reducing the mosquito population (let us say spraying oil on the breeding ponds) is still a less expensive method of obtaining a certain amount of mosquito abatement than is private spraying, but that the difference is small. This situation is illustrated in Figure 4. We assume that methods of mosquito abatement by collective means exist and these are efficient enough so that if all members of the community were compelled to contribute the cost of purchasing one unit of mosquito abatement, the cost would be ninety-five cents per head; whereas a private purchase of one unit of mosquito abatement would remain at one dollar. If we consider only Mr. B whose demand curve is shown on the diagram, clearly collective provisions would be desirable. He would be better off purchasing x units of mosquito abatement at ninety-five cents instead of purchasing b units at one dollar, which is his market economy alternative. His net benefit is measured by the areas shaded horizontally and slanting to the left in Figure 4.

If, however, we consider a community consisting of three members (Mr. A, Mr. B, and Mr. C), the situation becomes more complicated. Mr. A, for example, benefits from the lower price of mosquito abatement to the extent of the horizontally shaded trapezoid to the left. He is injured by having to buy more mosquito abatement than he wants to the extent of the vertically shaded triangle. He is in a worse position with collective provision than he would be with individual provision. Naturally, this simply reflects where we have chosen to draw his demand line, but we will be able to discuss the subject in a more general way after we have considered this example. Mr. C is affected in a somewhat more ambiguous way. His gross gain is the gross gain of Mr. B plus the dotted triangle. However, he suffers a loss to the extent of the triangle shaded by lines slanting to the right by not being able to purchase mosquito abatement privately. This loss will only be suffered if it is not possible for him (for technological or legal reasons) to supplement the public provision at the same cost as he could have previously bought mosquito abatement privately. If the public provision of mosquito abatement actually reduced the cost of additional mosquito abatement (which is conceivable), he may make an additional profit. If the public provision

23

made private supplements rather inefficient (which I imagine is the common case), then Mr. C would face a supply curve somewhat similar to the horizontal dashed line and would purchase c' — x mosquito abatement privately. The gross cost to him of the new arrangement then would be the trapezoid lying between the horizontal dashed line and the one dollar line. If this were a smaller area than the rectangle to the left of the new supply quantity, he would gain in net terms.

Let us turn to the question of whether it would be desirable to undertake public provision of the mosquito abatement for this small three-person community. If the provision of public abatement injures both A and C and benefits B, then the welfare economist would inquire whether B is able to compensate A and C for their injury. If (and this is also quite possible) the provision benefits both B and C but injures A, then of course it is more likely that compensation can be paid. Unfortunately, with public goods and with the quantity of public goods set by voting, or any other collective process, compensation becomes almost impossible in the real world.

Under these circumstances we will be unable to find out the amount of the compensation. Mr. A probably has not given much thought to how much would be required to compensate him for x mosquito abatement and the resulting taxes. If asked to give thought to this rather strange problem, he has absolutely no motive to correctly interpret his own feelings. This would be even more obvious if we were dealing not with our small three-man community but a larger unit. In the three-man community, A might feel that too large a claim for damages on his part may prevent the whole project. Thus, there would be some limit to how much he could exaggerate his loss. Similarly, B and C even if they benefit would probably find difficulty in placing a monetary value on their benefit and have substantially no motive to do so accurately.

As a general principle, attempting to get voters to compensate each other for their individual losses is not a feasible political proposition. Thus, we cannot use the traditional welfare method of making a direct payment from the people who gain to the people who were injured. There is, however, another and rather debatable tool in the welfare economist's toolbox. Some (but by no means all) welfare economists would argue that if we could compute that the payment would be possible, then it is not necessary to make the payment. Under this line of reasoning, if there is a computed net social benefit, we do not need to concern ourselves with the way in which it is distributed. This method of applying the Paretian criterion is highly controversial and I do not wish to endorse it here. There is, however, a variant on it which is clearly respectable.

According to this variant, if we anticipate making a large number of decisions in the future, and if we cannot tell who will benefit and who will be injured by any one of these collective decisions, but can anticipate that most members of the society will find themselves benefited sometimes and injured sometimes, then the rule of simply computing whether there is a net benefit or not and using that rule for all of these decisions would probably give to each individual in society a positive discounted future income stream. Applying this routine to our present problem, we may find that there was a net benefit for society as a whole.[11]

[11] For further discussion of this matter see Buchanan and Tullock, *The Calculus of Consent.*

Whether we would or would not depends on the particular values of various parameters and the preference functions of the individuals.

It could be said under this argument that if we found a "net gain," we could undertake the collective provision of mosquito abatement without worrying about the fact that some people (particularly Mr. A) are injured. Mr. A is injured, Mr. B is benefited, and depending on the particular parameters of the problem, Mr. C may be either benefited or injured. This transfer is clearly not something we would positively favor, particularly since the members of society who are interested in restricting the consumption of any particular public good are apt to be the poorer members. Thus, the income transfers we are now talking about are apt to be transfers from the poor to the better off. Poor Mr. A is made worse off, middle-class Mr. B is benefited, and upper-class Mr. C may gain or lose. Still this is not an absolute argument against collective mosquito abatement. Surely if the computed gain was very large, we would favor collective provision.

One further conclusion may be drawn from our discussion thus far. If collective provision of some good and private provision can be combined (that is, if the private provision can be used to supplement the public provision) there is an argument for reducing public provision. Mr. A can do nothing about the taxes that he must pay for x amount of mosquito abatement. If, on the other hand, the community provided only b, it would be possible for Mr. C to supplement this amount to some extent by private purchase. Thus, in cases of this sort we should provide somewhat less of the public good than otherwise, because it is easier to add additional units privately than it is to evade paying taxes. In general, the larger the cost savings, the more likely it is that we would choose collective provision; the more similar the different individuals demand curves, the better the collective alternative.

The basic parameters that have guided the decision between collective and private provision of mosquito abatement have been essentially technological. It is, therefore, sensible to pause briefly and inquire exactly as to the nature of technological superiority of collective provision in this case. At first glance one may think that it was simply an example of an ordinary scale economy, but this is clearly not so. General Motors has surely exhausted all the scale economies that are available in the manufacture of automobiles, yet we find no need for collective provision here. General Motors can sell its cars to people scattered all over the United States without worrying very much about whether the next-door neighbor of any given purchaser of a Chevrolet owns a Ford.

If we look at the detailed problems of mosquito abatement, we would also notice no significant scale economies. The private companies that manufacture the bug bombs for private mosquito abatement are probably characteristically considerably larger than are the companies that provide aerial spraying. Furthermore, the community of 1,000 that we are talking about is not a very large economic unit, and it is normally not large enough to be capable of providing the spraying itself. The community will characteristically turn to a private contract sprayer. This private concern, if it is an ordinary one in this business, will not only spray cities but will also spray or dust individual farms, mainly for pests other than mosquitoes. Thus, some individual citizens (farmers) are able to purchase this good, which for the small city we have been talking about becomes a collective purchase. Furthermore, the small city is not large enough to exhaust the economies of scale in a traditional sense.

The special characteristic of the aerial spraying of mosquito abatement is that it is generally impossible to spray economically on one city lot at a time. For economy, it is necessary to spray a fairly large area partly because the plane must fly from its airport to the place where it releases the spray and partly because the characteristics of the spray are such that it is apt to spread to several surrounding house lots. If only one householder is paying for it, the others will receive a "free ride." The problem, then, is geographical contiguity. As we continue, in the remainder of this book, we will find that geographical contiguity is a basic characteristic of almost all of the problems to which we will turn our attention. The distinction between an economy of scale that can be obtained only if the customers are located next door to each other, and an economy of scale that can be obtained without this type of contiguity, will be basic for our analysis. This is, of course, why these effects are so often called "spillovers," or "neighborhood effects."

# ( 2 )

# Property, Contract,
# and the State

A traditional scholar may be quite surprised by my beginning a discussion of the desirable role of the state with the topic of mosquito abatement. In a sense this surprise was my motive in so starting. The traditional approach does not seem relevant in discussing mosquito abatement and new methods are clearly needed. Furthermore, mosquito abatement is a particularly good example for introducing the newer techniques that have been developed in this field. The more general application of these newer techniques is the subject of this book. Today part of our society is market controlled and part is government controlled. This mixture has developed mostly without any scientific study of the desirability of placing any particular portion of the economy under market or government control. It simply developed in this way because the scientific tools for investigating the problem were discovered only very recently. In fact, this book will be the first attempt to make a *general* application of these newly discovered techniques to the problem of the scope of government.[1]

The new approach to government involves two strands, both discovered relatively recently. The first of these is "social cost, externality, and public goods," dating back to Pigou's *Economics of Welfare*.[2] The second, the application of economic analysis to the functioning of the government itself, is even more recent. Considering these two strands in combination is more recent still. Considering these two different lines of research and their interaction, and using them to determine the desirable scope of governmental and private action seems worthwhile.

It should be noted that in the present state of our knowledge it is impossible to reach final conclusions as to the exact portion of our society that should be governmental and that portion that should be market controlled. The field is new, and we need to perform empirical research to develop certain parameters that we do not now know. Until this research is done, no one can say with certainty exactly what should be left to the market and what should be undertaken by the government. Thus, to a considerable extent, this book will develop a theoretical structure to which it is hoped empirical research will eventually add an element of definiteness and precision that will make it possible for us to make decisions about the real world. In practice, I will express my particular views as to what parameters should be in some cases and thus draw actual conclusions. The reader should, however, accept this as

[1] Richard A. Musgrave in his classic book, *The Theory of Public Finance* (New York: McGraw-Hill, Inc., 1959), aimed at much the same objective. Unfortunately much of the research developed after he wrote his book. Hence his book suffered from "prematurity."

[2] Arthur C. Pigou, *The Economics of Welfare* 4th ed. (London: The Macmillan Company, 1938).

simply an expression of personal prejudice on the part of the author, and an effort to make the book less dry than it would be if it were entirely theoretical. These conclusions in general are not of any high degree of scientific value. The analytical techniques used, however, do seem to be sufficiently developed so that we can be fairly confident of them. Our problem in this area is not that our analytical techniques are poor, but that we have not yet accumulated the empirical information necessary to apply them.

It will not have escaped the reader that I have mentioned only two sectors of the economy: the private market and the government controlled portions. Most economies include a number of other economic areas, charity and non-profit activity, for example, or intrafamily relations. The boundary between these areas and the areas controlled by the market and the government is as important as the problem discussed in this book, but, I have very little to contribute on the subject. Research in these areas is relatively new and undeveloped. These sectors are less easily controlled by governmental policy than is the boundary between the government sector and the private sector. Nevertheless, a complete theory would also require a careful treatment of these areas. Unfortunately, we will have to wait a number of years for the theoretical and practical developments that will make it possible to produce a picture of society in which these additional areas are treated along with the government sector and the market sector.

The newer method of dealing with the market-government problem involves one philosophical change in our approach to government. In the Middle Ages, it was widely believed that both the economic side of life and the political side aimed at higher, transcendental goals. Since the time of Adam Smith, economists have, on the whole, assumed that the purpose of the economic sector was simply to carry out the desires of various individuals. These individuals might, of course, have desires that are not of a "selfish" nature; they might be interested in charity, glorifying Buddha, or a holy war. Nevertheless, the analytical technique used individual preferences and inquired as to how these preferences could be "maximized."

Most theorists of the state, however, retained the older view. The state was seen as a method of reaching some "higher goal," such as the "public interest," rather than simply a way of "maximizing" the preference schedules of individuals. Perhaps the reason for this was simply that most of the states in history have been despotisms of one sort or another, and maximizing the preference schedule of the despot did not seem a very desirable goal to the philosopher. For those of us who live in a democracy, this problem does not arise. Recent studies of politics, mainly by economists, have transferred Adam Smith's basic idea to the political sphere.[3] There are several reasons for the change, one of which, of course, is simply that the economists are accustomed to using this set of tools. More respectable, however, is the fact that it is very difficult to see why we should be interested in a higher goal unless we have some way of determining what the appropriate "higher goal" is. If the higher goal is somehow given to us, let us say in a book that we believe to be sacred, and does not require a detailed interpretation, then we could aim at maximizing it. In the real world, however, these higher goals invariably turn up as statements made by human beings; other human

[3] It should be noted that Adam Smith himself did not create the distinction. The development of different philosophical approaches to economics and political science is a later development. See Nathan Rosenberg, "Some Institutional Aspects of the Wealth of Nations," *Journal of Political Economy*, 68 (December 1960): 57–70.

beings favor other higher goals. Such statements are, in a real sense, simply statements by these individuals of their preferences if we define preferences as widely as the economist characteristically does.

Here, however, I must say one thing in order to be completely candid. It is my opinion that most human beings are (except within their families) to a very large extent interested in fairly narrow selfish goals. Note, that I do not say solely so interested. Clearly, most people have some charitable impulses and some interest in things other than mere personal aggrandizement. The point I am making is simply that the resources they are willing to invest in these goals are customarily very much less than the amount they are willing to invest to reach straightforward selfish goals. The problem is an extremely difficult one, but I have attempted a little empirical research in the strength of individuals' charitable impulses. If we measure the strength of people's charitable impulses or devotion to higher goals by what they say, the result would indicate a relatively selfless population. If, on the other hand, we inquire how much people are actually willing to sacrifice for these goals, all the admittedly rather poor measures that I have been able to develop thus far indicate that the amount is small.[4] Furthermore, the individual is not more charitably inclined in the political sphere than he is in the private sphere. Private individuals do make gifts to charity, but these gifts usually are only a small part of their income. The same individual acting as a voter will customarily vote for "welfare programs" that benefit people for whom he feels charitable impulses. Again, however, the amount of the national

---

[4] For measures, see Thomas R. Ireland and David B. Johnson, *The Economics of Charity*, ed. G. Tullock (Blacksburg, Va.: Center for Study of Public Choice, 1970).

budget that he is willing to allocate in this way is relatively small.

This analysis is somewhat obscured by modern budgetary accounting in which a very large share of the government's income will customarily be allocated to "welfare." If we examine this expenditure, we normally find that the bulk of it goes to people who are by no means poor. It seems likely that what actually happens is that the welfare expenditure is largely obtained by political pressure applied by its recipients. Mr. A may be interested in voting for a candidate who proposes to improve the well-being of the poor, but he is even more interested in voting for a candidate who proposes to improve his own well-being. The candidate who is able to combine these two and who announces a program that he says will benefit the poor, but also benefits Mr. A (and very likely benefits Mr. A much more than the poor) will get his vote. It is indeed even possible that no charitable impulses at all are expressed in voting. The entire aid that the poor do obtain, and they do no doubt obtain such aid, may be the result of the fact that they themselves can vote and, selfishly, vote for aid to themselves.

There are various bits of evidence that this last view might be the correct one. In most Western societies the poor actually do not receive any great amount of aid from the state. The bulk of the welfare program is expended for people who are well above the bottom 20 per cent in income, and the bottom 20 per cent remain in poor condition. Second, those people who are poor but do not have votes characteristically do very badly. The obvious case of this, of course, are those people who are aided only by foreign aid programs. Here we have a clear case of charity with the recipient not being permitted to vote. Most countries are not willing to invest much of the national income in this activity, although the poor in foreign countries are characteristically much poorer than the poor who have the vote inside the national boundaries of the Western democracies. Another example, which is of interest perhaps only to Americans, is the pay scale of draftees in the United States Army. The people who are drafted into the Army very commonly cannot vote because they are too young, and they are given a very low rate of pay. Seventy-one thousand military "heads of families" were, in fact, officially classified as living in poverty in 1966.[5] Thus we have a government that is allegedly engaged in a "War on Poverty" and yet that is paying some extremely important employees less than what it itself maintains is the minimum amount that any American should receive. It seems likely that the political reason for this action is that people are really not very charitable and that soldiers, many of whom do not have the right to vote, are unable to exert political pressures to obtain increased income for themselves. If so, this would be an illustration of the basically noncharitable nature of most governmental welfare expenditures.

This, however, has been a digression into what I consider the shape of people's preferences to be. I could be quite wrong, and it would still not invalidate much of the discussion in this book. As a matter of fact, the specific problem of the redistribution of income will be dealt with only in a chapter near the end of the book, and the earlier chapters will deal solely with cases in which government might adopt some policy, such as mosquito abatement, without much concern for its possible distributive effects.

To return, then, to our main theme, it will be assumed that the state (like the market) has no goal "higher" than the carrying out of the desires of the people who are

[5] Personal correspondence from Lucy Cifuentes, OS-ASPE Economist.

"within" it. Our analysis will be similar to that used by ordinary economists in that we will in general not worry about what the preferences of the individuals are. Some concrete examples will be used to illustrate various theoretical positions, and in these concrete examples I will assume various popular preferences. In general, my assumptions as to people's preferences will not raise many objections, but it must be admitted they are assumptions, and we would need further empirical evidence to be certain they are true or false. The main reason for making these assumptions is that it is somewhat easier to discuss these matters in terms of a specific problem than in purely abstract terms. A secondary objective will be to indicate the general outlines of what, given our present state of knowledge, would seem to be the type of activity for which government organization is desirable and that type of activity for which government is undesirable. The latter is decidedly a state of the arts objective. We can hope that with time and with further research we will have better results. Nevertheless, it is sensible to use the best information you have.

We find ourselves, then, in the same world the economist has lived in for a very long time. We have a great many people with a great many diverse desires. In order to obtain the economies from division of labor and large-scale production, individuals will not be given exactly what they want in every respect. Stating the matter more precisely, they can, if they wish, consume a candy bar that is made exactly to their specifications provided they are willing to pay an extremely high price for it. As a result of mass production, it is possible to produce cars that are not exactly adjusted to each consumer's taste, but that rather closely approximate a large number of consumers' tastes at much less than the cost of producing a set of individually de-

signed cars. We observe that generally the consumer prefers to pay the lower cost for a car that is not exactly to
his taste rather than let us say, $200,000 for a car designed
especially for him. We regard the lower priced car as actually meeting his preferences better than the higher priced
car because we include the price among the factors that
determine his preference.

The same problem arises in government. The government will not normally provide exactly what each voter
wants because it would be too expensive to do so. The
voter would prefer a somewhat standardized product at a
lower price to one costing more but being fitted exactly
to his requirements. It is, however, unfortunately true that
we can anticipate a good deal more uniformity in government supplied goods than in private goods because the individual in voting must of necessity vote for the entire community and cannot make an individual choice. If he votes
for a standard provision for the whole community, he will
receive a standard commodity. If, instead of a standard
provision for the whole community, a complex mixture of
various amounts and types of consumption for different
members of the community is offered for political decision,
then his vote will not only determine his own consumption,
but also the consumption of other people. Similarly, his
consumption will be almost entirely determined by other
people's votes. Under the circumstances, we would anticipate that he would have less accurate adjustment of his
consumption to his desires than in the market.

This situation does not indicate that we should not use
government provision. It simply is one of the costs in government provision that must be set off against the costs in
market provision. Other special costs are also involved in
governmental provision. The average person buying on the

market is not very well informed about the products and services that he buys. He is, however, characteristically much better informed than he is about the political alternatives for which he votes.[6] Furthermore, there seems to be nothing much that can be done about this difference. It is almost certain that our present methods of choice in the two fields lead to this differential in information.

It should, however, be pointed out that although it is inevitable that the individual in making a political choice will be less well informed than the individual making a market choice, and hence is more likely to be fooled or defrauded, the difference does not have to be as large as it is under present institutional arrangements. The recent investigation of political theory indicates that a great deal of our present political structure is inefficient simply because it is badly designed. It is something that just grew up, that came to us by tradition, and was never really thought out. We can make great improvement in its design and hence increase the desirable scope of governmental as opposed to private action. Speaking analogically, if the market in producing a particular line of services is 50 per cent efficient, and the government is 20 per cent efficient, we would choose the market. If, however, it is possible to raise government efficiency to 60 per cent, we would choose the government. It should not, of course, be overlooked that it may also be possible to improve the efficiency of the market.

Let us now end our discussion of general philosophy and turn to technical problems. First, we must consider an old problem—that of property. Let us begin by considering our remote caveman ancestors who apparently invented the

[6] See Gordon Tullock, *Toward a Mathematics of Politics* (Ann Arbor: University of Michigan Press, 1966), chaps. 7, 8.

concept of property.[7] An individual caveman, perhaps, would think of putting up a hut in order to obtain shelter from the rain. If, once he put up the hut, anyone else could occupy it, or alternatively anyone could pull it down because they wanted to use the wood for a fire, it is unlikely that the individual would invest much in building the hut. If, on the other hand, the man who builds the hut is given complete control of the hut from that time on, so that he can prevent any others from occupying it and/or tearing it down for firewood, then the incentives for producing such a hut are much greater.

It might be thought that the institution of private property would help the man who built the hut but injure everyone else. This is clearly true if we are only considering an existing hut. The man who built the hut is in a better position if he is "given property rights," which means complete disposition over the future of the hut, but surely his fellow tribesmen would be better off if they were given freedom to use it themselves.[8] If, however, we consider a general rule giving anyone who builds a hut the right to retain exclusive control over that hut, then this institution will substantially benefit everyone.

On the vertical axis of Figure 5, the net cost of the services of a hut to an individual measured in hours of work is shown. On the horizontal axis, is shown the benefit he derives from them. The slanting line is the usual demand curve, in this case the demand for the services of the hut.

[7] It can be argued that property is much older than the human race. It is certainly true that a great many nonhuman species, particularly birds, are real estate "owners." The issue of biological "property," however, is still to some extent an unsolved one and I would like to leave it aside.

[8] This is basically what is meant by property rights—control.

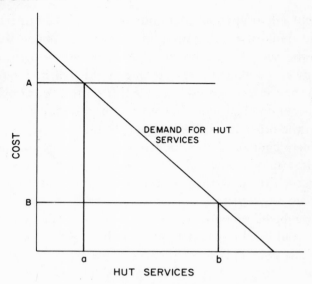

FIGURE 5. Demand with and without Property Institutions

Line A represents the cost of obtaining units of hut services assuming that there is no property institution, and line B shows the cost if there is property in huts. Note that the difference between line A and line B is not a difference in the cost of building the hut, which we assume is the same, but it is a difference, in essence, in the return on the investment. If I put one hour of my time into building a hut under the circumstances in which there is no property in huts, I can assume that as a result I will merely obtain the right to share the hut with other people until such time as someone needing wood for a fire pulls it down. Thus, although the hut is not very expensive to build, the hut services that I derive may be quite expensive. If, on the other hand, there is a property institution, putting one hour into building a hut gives me something that I can exclusively occupy, and gives me insurance that it will last as long as it does not fall down or I do not decide to tear it down. Under the first set of institutions, I choose a amount of hut, and under the second, I choose b amount of hut.

Note that under the nonproperty set of institutions, the individual would have some possibility of obtaining hut services from huts built by other persons. Presumably, the amount would be very low since the only incentive for building a new hut, which you would promptly have to share with everyone else in the tribe, would be that huts were scarce enough so that your right to, let us say, a one-tenth share in a hut for two weeks was worth more than the labor of building the hut.

In choosing between an individual opportunity set in which people are permitted to build huts for which they have permanent "ownership" or a set in which this institution does not exist, an individual would presumably prefer the first alternative simply because the existence of owned huts does not prevent the building of nonowned huts. In other words, he has greater freedom under these circumstances. However, we can go beyond this; we might consider two sets of institutions, one in which if you build a hut you own it whether you want to or not, and another in which you cannot own the hut. With this pair of institutions, it seems likely that the individual would prefer the ownership set, although judgment as to the shape of preference curves is required. Fortunately, it is a judgment with which I think very few people will quarrel. In a society in which anyone may tear down any hut for use as firewood, the individual would gain some benefit from the occasional construction of a hut by one of his neighbors, perhaps during a heavy rainstorm, thus simplifying both his shelter problems (because he could get into the hut) and his fire-wood problems later. Presumably, however, this would in most cases be a small benefit, much smaller than the benefit he could obtain from building a permanent hut himself.

The above description is the classical justification for property rights. It tells us that "property" is a desirable institution but it does not in and of itself tell us much about the desirable structure of this institution. Suppose, for example, that a primitive tribe has discovered fire. A man who has built a hut might be quite perturbed by someone else building a hut next door to his because the danger of the hut burning down is doubled. An accidental fire might occur in either of the two huts and spread to the other. Under these circumstances, I would be subject to an "externality" from a neighbor building a hut very close to mine. This is a "negative" externality; however, a possible "positive" externality might counterbalance it. The men of the Stone Age no doubt found the protection from marauders (human and animal) that came from having a large number of huts built very close together a benefit that more than outweighed the increased danger of fire. There would be an optimum location.

Externalities are innumerable and omnipresent. My choice of a necktie affects people I meet and therefore exerts an externality. If I choose to advocate or publicly oppose black power, this will affect the behavior of our society to some extent. If I vote for a politician because I think he will do something for me, the actions of that politician with regard to those who voted against him are, in essence, externalities. Returning to more characteristic economic areas, a factory that produces smoke involves an externality; the dumping of waste into water is an externality; loud noises are clearly an example of externality; and driving a car produces a large number of externalities ranging from the danger of life and limb to other people on the highways to the production of air pollution. Positive externalities are equally common. I may arrange my garden in such a way as to improve the view from my neighbor's house. Similarly, if I build a particularly attractive building for some purpose, this generates positive externalities for people passing by. The advance of science and technology creates massive positive externalities as well as the negative ones that are so often mentioned in the press. It should be noted that positive externalities can cause great deviation from the optimum because they are not extended as far as they would be if the beneficiary's interest were taken into account.

In addition to the danger of fire and the need for protection, cavemen may well have believed that some supernatural phenomenon made it important that all of the huts in the village have their doors facing north. If the doors were not all facing the north, then the hunting pole star would be annoyed. From our standpoint, this is fantasy, but if we consider their utility, they would feel injured by the construction of a hut with its door facing the south. What, then, can they do? The first suggestion is that an individual might simply pay his neighbors to choose a location for their huts that maximizes his utility. Note that this payment could either be positive, that is, he could give them a stone axe, or it could be negative—he could tell them that if they did not build their houses in the way he wished, he would smash their heads with the stone axe. In either event, he changes the choice situation that they face in such a way that they are more likely to choose as he wishes. We may examine this question in a very preliminary way with the aid of Figure 6. Assume that Gurt has a hut located somewhere and that Trug is thinking of building another hut due south of Gurt's hut. The only

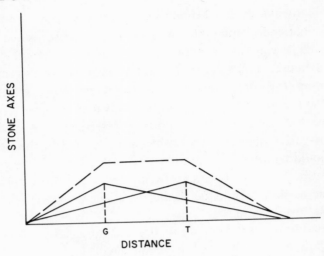

FIGURE 6. Preferences as a Function of Distance between Two Huts

question remaining is how far away Trug's hut will be. Gurt would prefer to have the hut at point G, and his preference slopes away from that point in both directions as shown by the line. We have shown the preferences in cardinal terms by inquiring how many stone axes Gurt would give to have the hut built at any given distance. If it is to be located very far away, he will pay nothing. Similarly, Trug has preferences as to the location of the hut and he would prefer to build it at point T. Here, again, his preferences slope away on both sides, and we have drawn in the number of axes he would be willing to pay for the "right" to put his hut at various distances from Gurt's hut.

These payments, according to the famous Coase theorem, are invertible. If Gurt would be willing to pay two axes to have Trug put his hut at point G, then two axes is also the price that he would be willing to take for permitting Trug to build it two miles away if Gurt had complete control of the location. Similarly, Trug would be happy to take two axes to build it well away from his optimum location. We can, in a sense, sum the two curves; that is, we can obtain the number of stone axes that the two people would pay jointly to build Trug's hut at some particular point, this sum being shown by the upper line. Note that this line is flat between points G and T, which simply indicates that I have drawn the original lines to make this phenomenon occur. If this were a traditional economic problem, we would probably predict that the hut would be built somewhere between points G and T and that there would be some compensation paid by one party or the other as the result of the bargaining. The exact location would have no welfare connotation. Unfortunately, as shall be seen in the next chapter on bargaining, such things are not simple. Nevertheless, we can use this very simple apparatus for our present purposes; note that if the two parties bargain, it is likely that the outcome will be better for both of them than if they do not. That is, contract is a way of reducing externalities.

Indeed, if it were not for the problems involved in bargaining, a contract would be a solution for all problems of externalities. Abstracting from bargaining problems, the optimum will always be reached by a system of freely arranged exchanges, provided of course that we are not concerned with income distribution. Unfortunately, the bargaining problem does exist and therefore this type of solution is not generally available. It should be kept clearly in mind, however, that private bargains are a major method of reducing or eliminating externalities. It should also be noted, as in the case of Figure 6, that it makes very little difference who is given the right to make the initial decision; if in the diagram Gurt had the complete right to determine where anyone else's hut was to be located, then Trug would have to pay him in order to move the hut away from point G. On the other hand, if Trug had the complete right to choose where to put the hut, then Gurt would have to pay him to move it away from point T. The location of the hut, however, would not be *very much* affected by this fact.[9]

In the real world we frequently observe private arrangements to reduce externalities. If I may give a rather extreme example, in the city of Orlando, where my mother used to live, a real estate man bought a plot of land intending to erect a commercial building on it. This would have required a change in the zoning code, which he thought would be easily obtained. In Orlando, Florida, as in most parts of the United States, the zoning code can be changed as a general rule only if the bulk of the neighboring property holders approve, and in this case they did not.

This annoyed the real estate man, who then built a most peculiar apartment house on the plot. It was not modern architecture; it was cheap architecture with a piebald paint job. Having this unsightly building, which needless to say was also poorly finished inside, he then proceeded to rent space in it to the most disreputable families he could find.

The result was quite amusing to those who did not live near it, and extremely annoying to the people who did. It was not a violation of the building code. The outcome, I

---

[9] Note the *very much*. The bargaining process may be affected by the point at which it begins. Secondly, the decision as to who has the power to make the initial decision and therefore must be bribed is in itself a decision about the distribution of wealth in the society. Since Gurt and Trug have different tastes, the decision that one or the other will have a larger amount of wealth should lead to somewhat different allocations. It is customary to leave these second order effects aside. This custom will be followed here, but the reader is at least warned that they exist.

suppose, was predictable. A number of neighbors joined together and bought the lot and apartment building from the realtor at a price that was found to be quite profitable to him. He had deliberately generated a negative externality that was eliminated by private contract. Note that in this case the externality was revenge for an externality generated by his neighbors who had used the local government to restrict his use of his land. Whether the outcome was or was not optimal was something about which I refuse to make a statement.

Further examples can easily be discovered. Last year I taught at Rice University, and as part of my teaching contract, the university required me to perform a few modest services, such as giving an occasional public lecture, which was designed to generate externalities of a positive nature for their principal customers, the students. This is a private contract. Similarly, I lived in an apartment building that enforced a variety of rules to prevent the individual apartment holders from annoying each other. On a more serious level, a very large number of economic enterprises involve "internalizing" externalities by private contract.

Fortunately, or unfortunately, according to your point of view, bargaining costs are not zero. In many cases the bargaining costs are so high that in ordinary speech we would say that bargains were impossible. We turn, therefore, to some type of collective decision-making process; that is, some arrangement under which individuals are compelled to carry out the wish of others. Thus we finally come to the role of the state, and this role superficially appears to be a very modest one—that of reducing the costs of bargaining. The reducing of bargaining costs may not be terribly dignified, but it is a matter of great practical importance in the world, and the states that perform this function tend to be very major and important parts of our society.

Suppose that each of the inhabitants of our Stone Age village had preferences as to the location of the other huts in the village. These preferences, we may assume, are not absolutely identical, although all may feel that if any hut is built with its door pointing south, this will injure the hunting for the entire village. If there were a general effort on the part of everyone to engage in bargaining with all the other people as to the location of all their huts, we could anticipate a tremendous amount of negotiation and bargaining, and no real prospect of a satisfactory outcome. Once again, if we look at the modern world we find this even more obvious.

Strictly speaking, nothing except bargaining costs prevents me from making an arrangement with a large number of other people under which we may privately build a network of roads. But when we say that nothing except bargaining costs prevents this type of action, we immediately realize how extreme these bargaining costs would be. The proposal that we replace governmental roads with an agreement to build roads privately is literally absurd. The full reason for its absurdity, however, oddly enough has only recently been discovered.

Activities of this type were traditionally handled by the government, and there was a realization that private persons could not undertake them, but it was not known that the reason private persons could not undertake them was simply that the bargaining costs would be excessive. There would be no way of assuring agreement within a finite amount of time. The development of government eliminates this problem. The outstanding characteristic of government is that we do not have to obtain everyone's agreement. Somebody makes a decision and then "pains and penalties" are applied to people who refuse to carry it out. These penalties have been different in different periods of history—at one time, boiling in oil, today perhaps something as minor as seizing a small part of a checking account. Furthermore, the government decision process itself has varied tremendously.

Probably, the most common governments under which human beings have lived have been despotisms. Characteristically these have not been benevolent despotisms, but disorderly and decidedly unbenevolent organizations. Nevertheless, if we observe history we see that most people much preferred to live under an inefficient and oppressive despotism to living with no government at all. This fact is an indication of the importance of the suppression of externalities and bargaining costs by even a very poor government.

We can, then, imagine Gurt and his fellow villagers deciding to establish a government that will issue rules on the location of the huts. Here we have two problems: (1) the nature of the government and (2) the nature of the rules that it issues. For the first problem, the nature of the government, we would expect from anthropological information about present-day tribes that the village would have some kind of chief who would usually seek advice from the other members of the village. This scheme, no doubt, would be better than having no government, but let us assume that our primitive community is in some respects very modern and that it reaches its decisions by a formal process of collective decision-making. It could vote on the decisions directly or it could elect some kind of council or even an individual to make the decisions. We need not

THEORY

consider here the question of whether each individual will have one and only one vote. In the real world this is, of course, a tremendously important problem; but for our purposes this decision is exogenous. For convenience we will normally consider a situation in which each individual has only one vote. Most of our reasoning, however, can be readily extended to other possible ways of voting.

The second problem is what kind of hut location rules the village (however it is constituted) should establish. Until very recently there were a considerable number of people who believed that the optimal way of running any economic organization (and house building certainly is an economic organization) was detailed regulation from the center. Clearly, this *could* indeed completely eliminate all externalities. As was demonstrated in the last chapter, however, a whole series of other problems was raised because individual preferences are subordinated to the collective decision. If you wish to optimize your own future utility stream, you would not want *all* of your decisions externally controlled, whether by majority voting or a benevolent authority.

In general this belief in detailed regulation has ceased to be a major intellectual influence in recent times, not because of the arguments that I presented in the last chapter, but because of a gradual realization that the detailed regulation is (with our present mental and physical equipment) impossible.[10] The advent of Liebermanism in the Soviet Union is simply one of the many chains of evidence that centralized planning does not seem to work. Furthermore, even if we looked at highly planned activities (for example, the Soviet Union before Liebermanism or the interior or-

[10] It is possible, although I think unlikely, that we may be developing apparatus that would make such detailed controls possible in the future.

50

ganization of some part of the government bureaucracy), we find a considerable use of decisions made outside the central planning office and "quasi-property."

If we look at any large governmental office, we find that the office furniture and a good deal of the office equipment is not kept in good order by detailed regulations. Such detailed regulations may exist, but the basic dependence is put upon what Alchian has named "quasi-property." I have been issued a desk and a chair by my university. If I am careless and scar the top of my desk by pulling things that have sharp undersurfaces across it, they will not fine me. They will simply leave me in "possession" of the same desk. Thus, I am motivated to be careful. This is an example of the sort of use of quasi-property that is common even in the most centralized and most highly controlled organizations.

Another, and more important, single subdivision of this same phenomenon, is the fact that in almost all large organizations, the head of any given office is given a good deal of discretion in dealing with various things within his area of control, and the restrictions on his decisions are not entirely in terms of general regulations, but partly in terms of making him continue to live with that office. These are examples of the use of quasi-property in the most centralized organizations. Today most people do not think that a high degree of centralization is desirable. Much of the recent efforts to improve the efficiency of government (particularly in the United States and particularly in the Department of Defense) have been attempts to create a decentralized process that functions somewhat like a market process although within a bureaucratic context.

But, be that as it may, most systems do have a mixture of property, government, and contract. The mixture is usually extremely subtle. For example, what is meant by property is characteristically a governmental decision. In fact, the government may be said to do more reducing of externalities by maintaining a law of property than by all its other activities put together. Similarly, it is sometimes very hard to see the difference between a contract and a government. The private corporation is clearly the result of a contract, a group of people entering into an agreement to conduct an enterprise.[11] They further agree to use some form of elective process to appoint the actual managers and give these managers control of the resources of the enterprise. It will be noted that if we just give the word "enterprise" a somewhat wider meaning, this description would fit Rousseau's theory of the state. It would also, I may say, fit my own theory of the state.

The corporation usually makes most of its decisions by a method other than unanimous consent. Exactly what method is used varies from time to time, from place to place, and from corporation to corporation, but clearly the decision-making process is not one of agreement by all interested parties. This permits much greater efficiency than requiring complete agreement and is the major reason why the corporate form of enterprise is adopted. We can find many other cases where individuals choose to voluntarily subject themselves to decisions over which they do not have a veto. Any club will serve as an example. Universities normally have rather obscure decision processes, but it is clear that total agreement is not necessary.

What, then, is the difference between a government and a corporation? The answer to this question is simply that

[11] Although in most cases the contract is closely regulated by the state, this is not necessary. There have been instances in which corporations have existed without corporation laws.

we have grown accustomed to calling one particular type of collective organization a government. Characteristically, there is one collective apparatus in society that is more powerful than any other and that can, if it comes to a battle, win over others. This apparatus we call the government. It should be emphasized, however, that the difference between this organization and a general contract is less than one might suppose.[12] Although it seems to me the difference between a corporation and the government is not as great as has perhaps been traditionally described, it still is true that there is much to be said for separately discussing the institutions of property, contract, and government. At the border, of course, it may be hard to tell in which of these areas any given institution should be classified. The government, for example, enforces contracts and both defines and enforces the laws of real property. Fortunately, for the purposes of this book, a precise distinction between these three spheres is not necessary. Most of the externality reducing institutions discussed will very clearly fall in one or the other of these three general areas and for those that do not thus classify themselves, the distinction will not be of much importance.

This book, then, will approach the classical problem of the scope of government from a modern angle. What should be controlled by the state and what should be controlled by private individuals either through contract or by themselves? In general, our method will be to contrast the externality cost to be expected through private action with the cost to be expected from government action. We will seek that combination of government and private action that optimizes the future discounted income stream of

[12] Cf. Thomas Ireland, "The Rationale of Revolt," *Papers on Non-Market Decision Making*, 3 (Fall 1967): 49–66.

members of society. Unfortunately, this approach is new and a great deal of empirical information necessary to make definite decisions is as yet unavailable. Thus, in many places the statements about the real world in this book are simply the conjectures of a reasonably well-informed observer. It is my hope that in a few more years it will be possible to replace these conjectures with carefully collected empirical data.

# ( 3 )

# Bargaining

Personally, I have always disliked bargaining and have been poor at doing it. This statement sounds peculiar coming from a man who at one time was an expert on China, but it is nevertheless true. It seems only candid to make this admission before I begin my discussion of bargaining so that the reader may be warned that I am an unsympathetic critic. I think, however, that the theoretical tools now available in economics are adequate and that my personal feelings are unlikely to result in any great distortion.

In an oriental bazaar, the shopkeeper will usually begin by asking a price somewhat higher than he actually hopes to get, but after some chaffering he and his customer will reach an agreement on the price and quantity. Economists have represented this situation by the standard Edgeworth box and have argued that the eventual outcome will be "efficient." This, of course, ignores the investment of re-sources in bargaining (an investment that I always object to). *Ex post* the parties would always be better off if they had reached the same agreement without investing re-

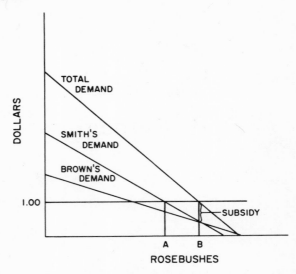

FIGURE 7. Individual and Social Demand for Rosebushes

sources in the bargaining. Furthermore, there may be enough friction in the process so that the neat economist's contract *locus* is not always reached. Nevertheless, this apparatus is clearly a reasonable approximation of reality.

Let us, however, consider a case in which there are externalities. Mr. Smith and Mr. Brown live next door to each other. Both of them have gardens and each can see the other's garden from his windows. If Mr. Brown put more resources into his garden, the view from Mr. Smith's dining room would be improved. The standard externality argument is shown in Figure 7. Mr. Smith has a demand curve for rosebushes in his own yard; Mr. Brown also has a demand for rosebushes in Mr. Smith's yard. These are illustrated in Figure 7, as is the cost of rosebushes (one dollar each). Now if Mr. Smith simply chooses the number of rosebushes he would wish to put in his yard, he will purchase quantity A. Mr. Brown, however, who also obtains some satisfaction from the roses, has a demand curve for rosebushes in Smith's yard, and if we add these two demand curves, we have a total demand curve. Point B, which is the global optimum number of rosebushes, can quite readily be obtained if Mr. Brown is willing to pay a subsidy equivalent to the marked triangle in return for Mr. Smith's planting the additional roses. The subsidy would be less than the gain for Mr. Brown, which is, of course, the area between A and B and under Mr. Brown's demand curve. Thus, both Mr. Brown and Mr. Smith could be better off by moving to quantity B with the making of a suitable payment by Mr. Brown to Mr. Smith.

In the real world, for various reasons, we do not observe such transactions frequently. One reason that certainly has some real importance is that gardeners may regard gardening as a competitive sport; although the view from Mr. Brown's dining room window would be more beautiful if Mr. Smith had more rosebushes, he actually prefers a view that permits him to feel superior to Mr. Smith. Although I am sure that this kind of jealous feeling exists, I do not believe it is universal, which leads us to the question of why this type of bargaining is not more common.

Through the use of Figure 8, we can develop an explanation for the absence of such bargaining. On the horizontal axis, I have placed the number of rosebushes in Mr. Smith's yard. Mr. Smith, acting independently, would choose the quantity indicated by "Smith's plan." Mr. Brown, however, could pay him a subsidy, which is shown by the vertical axis. If we consider the optima on this two-dimensional plane, Mr. Brown would prefer to have Mr. Smith put in more rosebushes voluntarily; so Mr. Brown's optimum is shown on the lower boundary to the right of Mr. Smith's

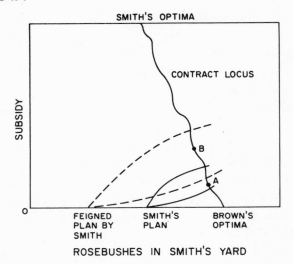

FIGURE 8. Bargaining on the Reduction of an Externality

plan. Mr. Smith, on the other hand, would prefer to put in the number of rosebushes, ignoring income effects, he originally planned and to also receive a large transfer payment from Mr. Brown. Thus, his optimum is at the top of the diagram. Note that the upper boundary on the subsidy that is shown in Figure 8 is there simply for convenience. There is no natural law limiting the size of the payment that could be made.

If we regard this diagram as a conventional bargain, we can then draw the indifference curves of Mr. Smith and Mr. Brown through Mr. Smith's plan, and bargaining between the two parties would then proceed until they reach some point on the contract locus such as A. If the "play" begins with Mr. Smith truthfully stating his plan, then there is no reason why this kind of bargaining should not occur. In the real world, however, Mr. Brown has no way of knowing Mr. Smith's actual plan. Thus, Mr. Smith could choose to announce the "feigned plan." The indifference curves through this are the dotted lines. The result of the bargaining might be that Mr. Brown would end up in a position like that of Point B, which is substantially worse than if he had never contemplated a subsidy.[1]

Under these circumstances, on the whole, Mr. Brown is unwise to begin negotiations, since the end product is likely to be that he will be worse off than he would have been if he had done nothing. Thus, not only does Mr. Brown waste his resources in the bargaining process, he may actually reduce his ultimate degree of satisfaction. This is, of course, not inevitable. He can make a gain, but clearly the situation is quite different from that of traditional bargaining in which the individuals each know the other's location at the start, and there is no doubt that they will move in the general direction of an improvement for each of them. The possibility open to Mr. Smith in our example of concealing his initial position, while Mr. Brown's initial position cannot, strictly speaking, be concealed, makes this type of bargaining highly one-sided and may lead to significant injury to Mr. Brown.[2]

In the real world we sometimes observe payments of one sort or another being made to change the gardening arrangements next door. If these happen intermittently so

[1] If Mr. Smith were to announce that his basic program was to plant the number of rosebushes shown at the feigned plan, then he would in a sense be presenting Mr. Brown with a set of indifference curves for which the contract locus would be farther to the left than the one I have drawn in. The bargaining might proceed to this contract locus instead of to the real one. But it seems likely that having reached this feigned contract locus, the parties could then go on to the real contract locus.

[2] It would not, of course, be possible for Mr. Smith to know exactly where Mr. Brown's optimum was, but he could safely assume that it was on the horizontal axis and to the right of his own.

that they cannot be anticipated, they may be reasonably successful. Perfect adjustment, of course, is not to be expected. As a simple example, Mr. Brown might one day come to Mr. Smith and say that he had been able to buy a half-dozen rosebushes at a great bargain and he only wanted three of them for his yard. He might then ask if Mr. Smith would like the other three. Probably Mr. Smith would accept the gift. If Mr. Brown did this regularly, however, Mr. Smith would begin planning his own purchase of rosebushes in anticipation of a gift and Mr. Brown would be worse off than if he had not provided the subsidy.

But with the clear possibility of gains to both Mr. Brown and Mr. Smith, we should carefully consider whether there may not be some method of avoiding these bargaining problems. For example, if Mr. Brown were to compute the exact value to him of each rosebush in Mr. Smith's yard and agree to pay Mr. Smith that amount, then the rosebushes would clearly be installed to exactly the optimal amount. Unfortunately, from Mr. Brown's point of view, it could amount to a large subsidy to Mr. Smith and he would presumably regard the net outcome as being worse than if he had done nothing. This loss would occur in spite of the fact that on the *incremental* rosebushes his payment would exactly balance his gains.[3]

Another possibility for Mr. Brown would be to make an estimate of what he thinks Mr. Smith will do and then offer a payment for rosebushes beyond that point. The problem, of course, is that Mr. Smith would have a strong motive to give the appearance of putting in fewer rose-

[3] See M. I. Kamien, N. L. Schwartz, and F. T. Dolbear, "Asymmetry Between Bribes and Charges," *Water Resources Research*, 2, no. 1 (1966): 147–157. A comment by Gordon Tullock together with a reply by Kamien, Schwartz, and Dolbear are printed in *Water Resources Research*, 2, no. 4 (1966): 854–855, 856–857.

bushes than he actually intended. Once again, we can readily imagine a situation in which Mr. Brown was worse off than he was before.

Altogether the possibilities of mutual gains through this type of bargaining seem poor. It is possible, however, that there is an arrangement that would help both parties. Let us suppose that Mr. Smith is also interested in the number of rosebushes in Brown's yard, which is surely not inconceivable. One can imagine an arrangement between Mr. Smith and Mr. Brown under which each of them agrees to pay, let us say, 10 per cent of the cost of planting rosebushes in the other's yard. If the two parties had a similar taste for rosebushes, there would be substantially no change in their wealth, but there would be a change in the marginal conditions under which they purchased rosebushes. Each would buy more rosebushes, and the appearance of the two yards would be more pleasing.

As far as I know, there are no examples of this kind of bargaining in the world. Perhaps one of the reasons for this is that the end product would certainly not be on the contract locus. Some kind of "rough and ready" system under which each party receives the same amount of subsidy would probably be necessary, and this would most assuredly deviate from the theoretical optimum. A second, and probably more important, reason may be that people feel that the benefits are not worth the time, and a third possibility is that people just have not thought of it. We tend to forget that there is such a thing as technological progress in contracts. People discover new ways of making agreements, and over a period of time we obtain considerable benefit from this sort of technological progress.

The possibility of implicit bargains of this type with a different institutional structure will be studied later in this book. For the moment, let us simply note that they do not often occur and that an externality in which one party wishes to change the behavior of a second party by the payment of subsidies leads to a bargaining problem of extraordinary difficulty. The problems are twofold. First, Mr. Brown is attempting to change Mr. Smith's behavior without any positive information as to what Mr. Smith's behavior would be if Mr. Brown did not make his attempt to change it. Mr. Smith has an advantage in the bargaining and Mr. Brown may not wish to enter into a process of bargaining that will quite possibly put him in a worse position than he would have been if he had never suggested the bargaining. The second, and more basic, problem is once again the problem of contiguity. In ordinary bargaining we know what the other party's reservation price is because we know what competing offers are available on the market. These offers give us a fairly good measure as to what we can expect from the man we are dealing with. In this case there is only one person living just north of Mr. Brown. This contiguity characteristic, the delimitation of the bargaining to one specific person or to a small contiguous group, is an important factor in the bargaining difficulties in this case. When we turn to multiple party bargaining, we will find once again that contiguity is a basic and major problem. If we could somehow shuffle pieces of real estate around, it would make a tremendous improvement in the functioning of both our market economy and that part of the economy that must be dealt with politically.

Perhaps we should note that the advantage that theoretically can be obtained from an agreement between Mr. Brown and Mr. Smith could, also theoretically, be obtained through a government agency that placed a suitable tax on Mr. Brown and used the money to subsidize Mr. Smith.

Unfortunately, again, there seems to be no way in which we can obtain the necessary information to make the proper adjustment. Mr. Smith would have no motive for correctly informing the government agency of his initial position. Mr. Brown, on the other hand, may wish to obtain profits on the deal and thus also misrepresents his preference curves. All that the government could hope for would be some kind of rule of thumb, which might well be better than what we would, in practice, obtain in the market, but would not be a perfect solution and would not obtain the total profit that can be made in theory from the situation shown in Figure 7. Here the bargaining problems are such that it is impossible for either the political or the market process to reach the theoretically optimal solution. Whether the market process or the political process would reach the best solution is a matter on which one can have opinions but no real knowledge in the present state of the world.

The real bargaining problem occurs when there are considerable numbers of people whose agreement is necessary. Once again, contiguity is the important problem because it necessitates dealing with a specified group of people. The problem that would arise if General Motors decided that it wished to buy up *all* of the shares of stock now outstanding in public hands is that they are held by a designated group of people. Every year General Motors sells automobiles to a group of people that is larger than its stockholders, but not having a designated group to deal with it finds this relatively easy. Generally, it is easier to sell 10,000 people out of 1 million than it is to sell 10,000 people out of 10,000. Indeed, it is probably easier to sell something to 10,000 persons out of 1 million than to 100 out of 100. In a normal "take over bid" in the stock market, the people buying control of the corporation reduce their total potential profit by not attempting to buy all of the stock. Their offer will be to buy at a specified price provided, let us say, that at least 85 per cent of the stock is tendered to them. They are aware of the fact that this gives the holders of 15 per cent of the stock a "free ride," but they are also aware that attempting to get all the stock would make the deal impossible.

Most cases in which governmental action is called for, however, are cases of contiguity because a certain designated group of people must be dealt with who live, own property, or work next to each other. The typical externality is "geographic." Let us begin our analysis of this problem with a matter that is not often a governmental activity by supposing that there is a tract of land now being used for housing on the outskirts of an American city. Assume further that there are forty people who have houses on the land with lots of varying sizes and characteristics. Let us also assume that at the moment the total real estate value of the lots on which these houses exist is approximately $100,000 and the houses themselves are valuable enough so that the value of the whole area (in its present use) is around $500,000 and that the location is very suitable for the establishment of a shopping center. If all of the lots are placed together in one unit, it is highly probable that the real estate alone can be sold to a developer for a price of $1 million. I should say that there is nothing even modestly improbable about this example.

Here we have a problem in what is called "assembly" of property. If these various individual plots can be grouped into one unit, they are much more valuable than if they are kept separate. Assembly of property is an extremely difficult and costly business. Most specialists in the field would look at the problem I have stated above and simply say that it was impossible to obtain this potential profit of $500,000. By this they would mean, in essence, that the bargaining costs would be considerably in excess of $500,000.

Now, why would an experienced man in this trade feel that it would be impossible to purchase these homes at well above their current market value? The answer is, of course, the bargaining problem; but in order to understand it let us look into the situation of one individual house owner. If he agrees to sell his property to the organization that is attempting to assemble the plot at a price above its value to him, he makes a profit. But in this case (at least theoretically) a much larger profit is available. He is in the position of a monopolist holding an essential resource. If he refuses to sell his plot of land, then the entire deal cannot go through. Let us assume that the property that he holds has a current sale value as a single lot of $20,000 and that the remaining people hold property with a current sale value (again not assembled) of $480,000. If the owner of this single plot gives his permission, the value of the entire property is raised by $500,000. His consent to the organization of the plots in one holding is in fact an asset, which, if he refuses to sell, can inflict an opportunity cost of $500,000 on the other parties.

The real estate developers have a good reason for not paying our individual owner of the lot $500,000; the reason being that every single householder there is in approximately the same position. We have a situation in which any one of these people (if he holds out long enough) could reasonably assume that he will obtain a very large advantage over the others. Although no one would really anticipate making the full amount, it would be true that the individuals who held out longest, who were least cooperative with the people trying to assemble the land, and who showed the least interest in getting their land into the assembled group, would make the most money. It is a situation in which the potential payoff is extremely high for obstructive tactics. With a considerable number of people on the plot, one can assume a good many of them will realize this fact and will be obstructive.

Furthermore, it should be noted that the payoff for obstructiveness increases as time goes by. As the people who are attempting to assemble the plot pick up options on individual pieces of property, the amount of their investment increases and the probability they will be willing to abandon the entire matter is lessened; the likelihood that any remaining property owner's consent will be decisive also increases to some extent. The individual who holds out to the end might conceivably make the full amount, $500,000, even if the people buying the options have been paying large fees up to this point. The reason is simply that at the very end the individual's decision does make a difference of $500,000 to the buyer, and hence these people might be willing to pay it. One would also anticipate that the holders of the other pieces of real estate might be willing to make payments to him if the company assembling the property is not. Granted that the operation must take time, it is perfectly possible that the total payments made by the people who are trying to assemble the property will greatly exceed the value of the plot, although at any given time, their estimate of returns on future expenditures is positive.

As I have said, with the number of people I have chosen to use in my example, most real estate assemblers would not be willing to undertake this particular operation. They probably would be quite willing to undertake it if the profit were as large as this and the number of people whose consent was needed was much smaller, but in general, if the number of individual owners is large, it is impossible to assemble land. This is part of the theoretical justification of the federal government's urban renewal program. It is argued that various areas of "deteriorated" property in the downtown areas of American cities cannot be revived by private persons. The reason, according to this argument, is that no individual would be motivated to improve the building on his property because the dilapidated buildings on adjoining property would make it impossible for him to rent or sell his property at a reasonable price. Thus, what is needed is a large plot of land that can be renovated at a single time.

If this argument is correct, the plot of land once assembled would be worth more than it was when disassembled because it is possible to avoid these externality effects. The impossibility of assembling the plot by private bargaining for the reasons outlined above is accepted, and it is therefore proposed that the government use its power of condemnation to force people to sell at what is normally called a "fair price," but that is usually (not always) a price that is somewhat above the market value. Clearly, there is nothing wrong with this argument. It is perfectly possible, although there have been a number of investigations in recent years that would seem to indicate that empirically the situation called for is not very common. It would seem that people are not as concerned with the appearance of buildings on neighboring plots of land as had been thought, so that the externality is smaller. Nevertheless, it is clear that a case can be made and regardless of whether or not we are in favor of urban renewal, it fits our specifications for government action.

One can continue to find innumerable other cases in

which it is perfectly clear that individual activity on one piece of property may create externalities (positive or negative) for people on the next piece of property and hence where the bargaining difficulties would be very great. The obvious case for this, of course, is national defense. In general it is impossible for someone who sets up an antimissile defense for a house in a city in which I am living to avoid giving me protection even if I do not choose to pay for it. Thus, the bargaining problem here would involve the entire population of the city, and it is extremely unlikely that it could be solved by voluntary contract.

The importance of these bargaining problems for the justification of government activity is, I take it, now clear. The externalities that governmental activities are mainly aimed at eliminating could be effectively eliminated by private bargaining, if it were not for the extreme difficulty involved in bargaining.[4] We do not turn to private bargains because of the extreme difficulty in bargaining in this area. The bargains would be extremely costly, and would take tremendous amounts of time, and to all practical intents and purposes can be said to be impossible. The pure theorist, of course, will insist that if one waited an infinite amount of time and were willing to invest vast resources into active bargaining, some agreement would eventually be reached.

Note, however, that there is a cost to government action. Bargaining will eventually reach the contract locus or the Paretian frontier; governmental activity will not. In fact, as we will demonstrate in Chapter 5, there is every reason to believe that governmental adjustment will characteristically be far from perfect. Thus, we would normally wish

[4] I am, as I mentioned before, deferring problems of income equalization until a later chapter.

to impose upon parties a certain amount of bargaining, rather than the use of governmental activities, simply because the bargaining will ultimately reach a conclusion that is superior to the government outcome. If the bargaining costs involved rise above some point (a point that at the moment we can not accurately specify but with further research we may know very well), then government becomes a more desirable way of dealing with the problem than does the private market.

The choice is one between two instrumentalities both of which have considerable error, noise, and inefficiency inherent in them. We choose between two imperfect instrumentalities and thus must face much the same situation as the mechanical engineer who must choose the power for a new ship. Since no engine is perfect, he chooses the one that, for the particular use concerned, is least inefficient. We will be doing the same. There is no reason why we should be particularly unhappy about this, but it is the choice between imperfect instruments rather than, as is sometimes suggested, the abandonment of an imperfect instrument, the market, for a perfect instrument, the government. The situation is rather analogical to the second law of thermodynamics, a general proof that no perfect machine can ever be produced. In any event, this book accepts the absence of a perfect institutional solution.

Bargaining costs are not only important as a reason for government action but they are also important in government action. If we observe any functioning government unit, we will always observe a great deal of bargaining between different parts of it, and between it and the general polity, whether this general polity consists of the voters or a central organization, as in the Soviet Union. This bargaining is also subject to the same costs as private bargaining, that is, it moves toward a contract locus that is a superior situation for the parties, and that it may be impossible to attain that locus within a finite amount of time.

In the particular case of government action, we characteristically have a situation whereby compensation is extremely difficult to arrange. Let us suppose that we have a simple majority voting rule and that the parties are not all equally intense about their views on some particular subject and/or we do not have single peak preference curves with respect to this subject. Under these circumstances, side payments in cash would be the economist's normal prescription. The people who are injured would then be paid off, and some citizens would benefit. As we have emphasized before, there is no reason why the individual should tell other people his attitude in such detail that we can compute the amount of side payments to make. Bargaining would be necessary under highly unfavorable conditions. The government could not compensate the people who are injured by its actions in any reasonably efficient way simply because extreme bargaining problems would be involved in determining how much compensation should be paid. Thus bargaining costs are both a reason for government and one of the reasons why it will never be perfectly efficient.

# ( 4 )

# Externalities
# and All That

The usual case of an externality in economic texts is a contract between two persons that will have some effect on a third person. I purchase a necktie; the salesman will seldom if ever see me wearing it and hence is not likely to be offended if I have bad taste, and I am presumably perfectly happy with the necktie (which I also will seldom see when I am wearing it). Those people who may see me and find it offensive, however, have no way of expressing their opinions at the time of the transaction. Note, however, that this is merely a standard example. If I were to make the necktie myself out of materials that I had raised with my own hands, only one person would be involved, but the effect on other persons would be the same or, perhaps, worse. Thus we would have an externality in this case, too. Similarly, there might be more than two parties to the original transaction. As long as one person who is affected is left out of the group whose consent is necessary, there is an externality.

The problem that most economists have examined in

their analyses of externalities has been the quantity of something or other purchased, not the exact specifications. Thus, you will find little discussion of the possibility that I might buy a red necktie, whereas I should buy a gray one. This tradition in the analysis of externalities is harmless since any qualitative problem can be converted into several quantitative problems. Thus, if I am intending to purchase a red necktie, and you would rather that I purchase a gray one, you can say that I am overinvesting in red neckties and underinvesting in gray neckties, and that it is the quantity of red neckties, that is, one, and quantity of gray neckties, that is, zero, which I am purchasing that disturbs you. This is simply a different way of expressing the same thing. Since this analysis of externalities is convenient, we will use it for the bulk of this book.

Externalities can arise either from action or failure to take action. The analytical tools needed to deal with an externality fortunately are such that action and inaction are easily handled with the same apparatus. Indeed, as a general rule, even the number of people involved in the externality is not of much significance in the analysis.

Let us begin with the classical case of the smoking chimney and temporarily assume there are only two people concerned: the factory owner whose chimney smokes and the next-door neighbor who likes to air her laundry on a line and finds that the smoke makes it dirty. Under these circumstances it has been demonstrated that, distributional matters aside, it makes very little difference what the initial situation is. Let us suppose, for example, that the law provides that factories may make as much smoke as they wish. Under these circumstances, the housewife would be motivated to offer a payment to the manufacturer to reduce his smoke emission. If the reduction of smoke by one unit was less costly to the manufacturer than the benefit conferred on the housewife, the amount that she offered him would be sufficient for him to reduce his smoke production until such time as the marginal cost to the housewife and cost to the manufacturer were equal. Similarly, if the law provides that the factory may not emit smoke without the permission of the housewife, the manufacturer could purchase the housewife's permission to emit smoke until such time as he reached the point where the two costs were once again in equilibrium. One would anticipate exactly the same amount of smoke from both of these institutional arrangements.

Since, however, this problem involves an effort by one individual to modify the behavior of another, the bargaining problems discussed in the two-party case at the end of Chapter 3 would be relevant here also. The manufacturer and the housewife would attempt to deceive each other as to their initial position in the bargaining game. In this respect, the housewife is at some disadvantage, because it is perfectly clear that her ideal is zero smoke. It would not be obvious to the housewife how much smoke the factory would emit if no payment were made, and hence the manufacturer may be able to deceive her in the bargaining process. She *might* end up worse off than she would have been if she had made no payment at all.[1] On the other hand, if the housewife is given the right to exact a payment from the factory owner for emitting smoke and the factory is already in existence, she may designate her price for emitting smoke high enough so as to extract the full rent on the

[1] M. I. Kamien, N. L. Schwartz, and F. T. Dolbear, "Asymmetry Between Bribes and Changes," *Water Resources Research*, 2, no. 1 (1966): 147–157. A comment by Gordon Tullock together with a reply by Kamien, Schwartz, and Dolbear are printed in *Water Resources Research*, 2, no. 4 (1966): 854–855.

existing factory from the manufacturer. Clearly he cannot operate the factory without emitting at least a certain amount of smoke from his smokestack and by prohibiting him from operating until he made a suitable transfer to her, the housewife could extract quite large amounts of money from him. It should be noted, however, that she will be best off if the factory produces at the point where the injury inflicted on her by the last unit of smoke is equal to the marginal cost of smoke reduction to the manufacturer. At this point she can obtain the largest total transfer from the factory owner. If the housewife has certain long-term goals, that is, an interest in attracting other industries to operate near her home, she might not extort this additional transfer from the factory owner.

If we wish to achieve theoretical perfection, this case presents a special difficulty. Not only is it necessary that the factory owner be charged for the smoke he emits, it is essential that the housewife somehow have her income vary with the amount of smoke damage. Suppose, for example, that we compute the cost to the housewife of each unit of smoke and place a tax on a factory owner of that amount, with the result that the factory owner reduces his production of smoke to the point where his marginal cost and that of the housewife exactly match. We do not, however, pay this tax that we have collected to the housewife. Under these circumstances, she would still find that there was a substantial smoke nuisance and might decide to purchase a dryer that she would not otherwise have wanted. This would mean that she would be suffering something in the way of an excess burden from the smoke emitted by the factory and hence society would still be receiving some injury from the smoke. Only if the housewife is subsidized to compensate her for the smoke injury do we obtain total optima.

Nevertheless, it may well be that a tax on the smoke without any payments to the householders would be a desirable social institution. The government must obtain money from some source, and the excess burden associated with the failure to pay the subsidy to the householder may be less than the excess burden obtained from other types of revenue devices.

In practice, of course, there is no reason to believe that a democratically selected tax would match the margins in the way we have been specifying thus far. It presumably would be higher or lower than the ideal tax depending upon the voting process. Nevertheless, a tax (even a rather badly calculated tax) may result in improvements. We must, however, keep in mind that a tax on the smoke may do considerably more harm than good. Once again the problem is not that of eliminating the externality by transferring the activities of the government, but that of comparing the inefficiency that arises from the externality in the market process with the inefficiency that arises from the decision procedures used in the government.

The inefficiency that can come through government can arise from a number of causes, most of which are to be discussed in Chapter 5. There is, however, one example that is a pure externality and, therefore, is best discussed here. Let us suppose that the factory produces smoke that blows over a fairly wide area. If the governmental unit that is to make the decisions on the factory's emission of smoke is exactly coextensive with this area, then all of the externality will be internalized to that district. The amount of smoke injury suffered by different pieces of property will vary, however, and the particular restrictions that will optimize the situation for one householder will not optimize for another. As we have pointed out before, compensation within the political process is not possible here, so it is likely that the outcome will be nonoptimal for this reason alone. There are, of course, a large number of other reasons, but even if we assume that all of the householders are perfectly informed and have some method of expressing their opinion that is free from defects, we would still anticipate that the tax placed upon the emission of smoke would be too heavy from the standpoint of some of the householders and too light from the standpoint of others. This is a fairly straightforward cost arising out of the political process.

The point of this short discussion of externalities, however, is not to deal with this specific problem, but with a more general example of the same thing. Let us suppose that the jurisdiction within which the factory is located does not encompass the entire area in which the smoke damage occurs. The individuals voting to establish an appropriate tax rate on the factory would have two objectives in mind. First, they would prefer, insofar as possible, to transfer income from the factory owner (and his customers) to themselves. This is, of course, a characteristic of substantially all political taxation schemes. Second, they would be interested in adjusting the production of smoke in the factory to the point where the marginal costs of introducing further smoke reducing procedures is the same as the marginal cost from additional smoke. This is the point at which they, granting that they are obtaining maximum practical transfers from the factory owner, will find their well-being optimized. Note, however, that there is no reason why the citizens of this district should take into account the well-being of people outside the district who would also suffer smoke damage. Therefore, the total smoke damage cost will not be "internalized," and the factory will emit more smoke than it should.

Let us, however, take the opposite case. Suppose that the governmental unit having jurisdiction over the factory is markedly larger than the area in which the smoke damage occurs. Under these circumstances, a considerable number of voters in the district will suffer no smoke damage at all. For them the tax will simply transfer resources from the factory owner to themselves. Clearly, they can place a higher tax on the factory owner without driving him out of business if he is permitted to emit more smoke. Since the smoke does not damage them, and since they have at least some influence over the political apparatus, one would anticipate a tax so arranged as to lead once again to a larger amount of smoke generation than is socially optimal.

Logrolling, of course, could eliminate this effect. It would give the people who lived closest to the smokestacks a disproportionate weight in deciding on restrictions. Unfortunately, here again there is no reason to believe that the social optimum would be achieved. The degree to which the externality is reduced, which may, of course, be more or less than the optimal amount, is extremely sensitive to the specific political arrangement that is used to deal with it. It is difficult to comprehend how a political organization could be motivated to establish the optimal size and organization of a political subunit to deal with an externality problem. Hence, it is likely that externality problems will be dealt with by political organizations that will normally not be ideal for dealing with the particular problem. Thus we can anticipate that some pure economic externality will remain even if we ignore the problems of political efficiency.

In pure theory the citizens who live close to the mill could join together and pay their more distant neighbors enough so that the voters would adjust the amount of smoke emitted by the factory and the tax collected from the factory to the social optimum. Once again this involves a highly unlikely bargaining process within the political process. Thus, perfect adjustment requires that the political area that makes the adjustment be exactly the same size as the area of the externality. But most externalities do not have a clear cut border; they do not inflict a five-dollar a year damage on every house out to some line and then zero. Thus, this is essentially an impossible requirement. The fact that most externalities gradually taper off so that the cost is different to different people means that any democratic process will almost certainly put an inappropriate level of taxation on the externality. The converse, of course, applies in those cases of externality that generate benefits rather than inflict injuries.

Note that there is no argument here that the government may not be able to produce a better outcome than the market. The point is simply that the government does not produce a perfect outcome. It is even possible to imagine circumstances where there is a very substantial externality, but where government activity would lead to a worse outcome than the market.

There has been a general tendency to ignore the externalities generated by the governmental process itself. These externalities can be classified in two categories. The first is the injury inflicted on me as a citizen of a state because the state does something I dislike. Let us say that I am deeply antagonistic to the Vietnam War; I object to the war itself and to paying taxes to support it. Nevertheless,

I find myself being compelled to participate. There are economists who say that this is not a true externality and there is no point in bandying words. They can call it by some other name if they wish, but I would be happier if I could prevent this situation from arising. The second type of externality arises because the government is engaging in some activity or failing to engage in activity that affects people outside its jurisdiction. It is fairly certain, for example, that the inhabitants of North Vietnam found the presence of large numbers of American aircraft flying over their country and dropping bombs a very, very prominent example of a negative externality. The cases mentioned previously in which the amount of coal smoke generated was inappropriate because the area of the governmental unit was inappropriate are simply milder examples of the same phenomenon.

Our present discussion involves only negative externalities, that is, externalities that inflict injury. This is not because they are the most important. On the contrary, I suspect that the so-called positive externalities are more important in the present-day world than the negative externalities, but the latter happen to be somewhat easier to handle analytically and anything that can be said about them may be transferred to positive externalities. The externalities I would like to discuss now are the so-called reciprocal externalities, which occur when A's activities affect B, and B's activities affect A. The factory chimney and the housewife are clearly an asymmetrical case. If we think of a number of people living in a community, all of whom burn soft coal and all of whom hang their laundry outdoors to dry, we have a case of reciprocal externality. Each individual would find that his laundry was cleaner if the amount of smoke he emitted was reduced. If he could persuade his neighbors to reduce their emission of smoke without reducing his own, he would be better off than if he was also compelled to reduce his own smoke emission, but normally this is not a politically feasible solution.

Situations that give rise to this kind of reciprocal externality are endemic in the present-day world. Probably the most conspicuous example is traffic congestion. If I decide to travel southwest on the Southwest Freeway between the hours of five and six in the evening, or to travel northeast on the same freeway between the hours of eight-thirty and nine-thirty in the morning, I will take into account the private costs of making this trip. One of these costs is that I will make a comparatively slow trip because of the number of other cars on the highway. Unfortunately, there are a number of other costs, which, if I am rational, I will not consider. The presence of my car on the highway increases congestion and therefore inflicts costs on the other people also on the highway. I have a choice, for example, between driving from my office to the Post Oak section at four o'clock in the afternoon or at five-thirty. I know that I will make a much quicker and more convenient trip at four than at five-thirty, but it will be inconvenient in other ways. Let us say that the benefit to me in terms of reduced wear and tear on my nerves of driving at four as opposed to five-thirty is two dollars, but the other inconveniences of leaving my office early would be worth two dollars and fifty cents to me. Under these circumstances, I would wait until five-thirty to begin my trip, but it may well be that the cost inflicted on other people by the presence of my car on the highway at that time is as much as fifty dollars to one hundred dollars. Thus, I am ignoring an externality and inflicting very substantial injury on other people.

Note, however, that all of the other people on the high-way at five-thirty are doing the same.[2] Under these circumstances we have an interesting situation in which a tax on everyone can make everyone better off. Let us suppose that the city of Houston established toll booths at the entries of the highways and charged a fee of one dollar for driving west on the freeway between the hours of four-thirty and six o'clock. This means that the number of people driving on the throughway at that time will be reduced. If I switch times and drive at four, the people actually on the highway will in net be benefited by the tax. Those people who do not drive on the highway are not benefited by the tax. In fact they suffer an excess burden, but it is probable that they are compensated for this by the government revenues derived from the tax. Thus we have what appears to be black magic: the people who actually pay the tax are not in any way injured by it; in fact, they achieve a substantial benefit. Even ignoring the revenue derived, by paying the tax and using the highway in an uncongested state, they are better off than they would be if they did not pay the tax and had to face the congestion. The only people who are injured are those who do not pay the tax. Clearly, their injury cannot exceed one dollar and should be much less. As an even more magical example, John Moore has examined the situation that would arise if all of the users of the highway simply reduced their consumption of it as a response to a tax. In this case there are no people who actually stop using the highway, and therefore there is no excess burden. Every

[2] There may, of course, be some individual on the highway for whom the advantage of driving at that particular time is great enough so that even socially he is justified in driving at that time. I rather doubt it, but it is possible.

single person can be directly benefited under these circumstances by a suitably chosen tax.[3]

Although the case of reciprocal externality is usually discussed in terms of many many persons, that is, congestion problems, it can arise with two people or a very small group. The reader will recall the case of two adjacent houses, with each owner interested in the number of rosebushes in the backyard of the other. Under these circumstances, it *may* be possible for the two parties to benefit themselves by entering into an agreement that eliminates the reciprocal effect of their choice of what they plant in their garden. As a result of bargaining problems, they can never hope to reach perfect adjustment, but nevertheless they may be able to effect a positive improvement in their welfare. In our previous example, each agreed to pay 10 per cent of the cost of rosebushes placed in the other's yard.

Nevertheless, the common case of reciprocal externalities is one that involves a large number of people. Moreover, reciprocal externality is, in general, the situation that will arise if some particular service can be provided cheaply if it is provided for an entire geographical area, and is extremely expensive if the individuals attempt to provide it by themselves. Our mosquito abatement project will serve as an example. Other examples are national defense and police. In each of these cases, there is no reason why a person would not hire his own services except that there are contiguity-scale economies that make this extremely inefficient.[4]

---

[3] See "Congestion and Welfare—Comment," John Moore, *The Economic Journal*, 78 (March 1968): 157–165.

[4] In general, these cases are discussed under the rubric of "public goods." A public good is defined as one that can be consumed by one person without any reduction in the quantities available to others. Thus my consumption of national defense does not reduce your consumption. In fact, they are simply extreme and rather special cases of an external-

I can, for example, hire a private policeman to pass in front of my house as often, or more often, than the city police do. It is also by no means impossible for me to spend part of my fortune on arms to protect myself against foreign enemies. In both cases, however, on the whole it is unlikely that I will obtain anywhere near as good results with this activity as does the government.

Furthermore, in all of these cases, it is highly likely that an individual who chooses not to protect himself in this way would find himself benefited to some extent by the protection purchased by his neighbors. If I hire a police patrol that will pass in front of my house (let us say) seven times a week at random intervals, and the police patrol observes a suspicious character three houses down from mine, that patrol would be protecting me rather poorly if it did not stop and question him. On the other hand, if it does stop and question the suspicious character, it is extending protection to people who have not paid for its service. Therefore, there is no obvious reason why my neighbor should choose to invest in protection if I am doing so.[5]

This is an example of the prisoner's dilemma. Let us say that hiring a police force having a reasonable degree of

ity. Furthermore, they are not necessarily publicly provided. A private television station is a similar example. It would be fantastically expensive to provide the type of entertainment that is obtained on television for a single user, but it is relatively economical if a large number of people share the services of the same station.

[5] Theoretically, it would be possible for this situation to be remedied by keeping a list of people in the vicinity who are and who are not protected, and permitting professional criminals to prey on those who are not protected. The reason that this would work, however, is not that it solves the externality problem but simply that the costs of being unprotected would be so high that one could predict that no one would choose to not pay. The amount of protection that should be given and its spatial arrangement would still be matters that could not be determined in this simple way.

efficiency would cost each individual ten dollars a year. If I refuse to contribute my yearly allotment, I will receive almost as much protection as if I did make the contribution. The problem is identical to that of the mosquito abatement program. Clearly the difference in my police protection will be only very slightly affected by my ten dollar investment, and I would, on the whole, be wiser not to pay. On the other hand, if everybody made this calculation, we would have no police force and thus would all be worse off than if each paid the ten dollars. Therefore, we join together and form a police force that has as one of its duties coercing people into paying the ten dollars. All of us are better off, although our freedom has been restricted.

The problem is simply a special case of a reciprocal externality. Gains can be made by collective arrangement for some particular service. It should be noted that the necessity for collective control of this particular service does not mean that it must be directly provided by a governmental body. A great deal of "governmental" activity is actually provided by private companies by contract or purchase. One of the suburbs of Houston has entered into a contract under which a private company provides its police force. More commonly, many small governmental units have entered into contracts with other governmental units under which the second governmental unit provides some service for the first in return for a fee. At the moment, we do not have any adequate criterion for the types of activity that should be provided directly by the government and the types that should be obtained by contract. The analogous problem in private industry, whether a company should buy or make components, is also extremely difficult.

A fairly good theoretical rule emerges for the types of "goods" that the government should purchase for its citizens. Stated more concretely, we have good arguments for the existence of a collective body that levies taxes in order to provide police protection. At the moment we have no arguments for that police force being provided through the direct hiring of individuals as policemen by the government, instead of entering into a contract with another governmental unit or a private corporation to provide the police force as a unit.[6] The fact that we do not now have a theory in this area does not, of course, indicate that none exists or that there is no reason why the entire government should not be contracted out to private persons. All we can actually say is that at the moment we do not know the answer.

To return to the pure problem of externality, generally speaking it is a matter of some importance that the externality be fully understood and the institutions designed to deal with it be carefully designed. For example, let us consider the factory with the smoking chimney. Suppose further that the householders in attempting to deal with the smoking chimney, instead of placing a gauge in the chimney and taxing the factory in terms of how much smoke it emits, taxed the output of the factory. Mistakes of this sort may not seem very likely, but as a matter of fact, on a somewhat more subtle level they can and do occur. Under these circumstances, the factory owner would usually reduce production, but the social optimum would be almost impossible to reach.[7] The factory owner is not impelled to

[6] Needless to say, in such contracting arrangements it would be necessary to avoid the prospect of a monopoly supplier. Normally this would cause no great difficulty. See Harold Demsetz, "Why Regulate Utilities?" *Journal of Law and Economics*, 11 (April 1968): 55–65.

[7] There are special circumstances in which a tax of this sort might both restrict output and increase smoke. I doubt that these special circumstances are likely to be met in the real world, but the theoretical possibility should be kept in mind.

invest his resources to reduce smoke emission but to restrict production as a whole. From the standpoint of the people who are attempting to adjust the output of smoke, this is not a completely irrelevant objective since restriction of production will normally reduce smoke. It is, however, a situation in which the adjustment is only indirectly relevant to the problem. The ultimate outcome presumably would be social waste; probably less than the original smoking chimney, but conceivably more.

An even more perverse effect can be obtained if some externality is produced in a joint production function with something else that has no external effects and a mistake is made in attempting to correct the problem. James Buchanan and I presented a case of this type in "Public and Private Interaction under Reciprocal Externality."[8] Contagious diseases produce an externality in that the individual who is ill may pass the illness on. As a general rule, individuals can deal with contagious disease in two ways. They can have themselves inoculated against it, and they can undergo medical treatment if they catch the disease. Reduction of contagion and reduction of the risk to other people largely depend on the former, since most diseases are contagious before they become serious enough for the person who has contracted a disease to realize that he should see a doctor. In present-day circumstances he is unlikely to pass the disease on while under medical supervision.

Thus, the inoculation reduces the likelihood that the individual who is inoculated will become ill and also reduces the likelihood of other people becoming ill. The individual presumably will not take the second effect into account, and therefore an externality is present. Govern-

---

[8] *The Public Economy of Urban Communities,* ed. Julius Margolis (Washington, D.C.: Resources for the Future, Inc., 1965), pp. 52–74.

mental action can readily be supported in this case. Let us suppose, however, that the government makes a mistake. It provides free hospitalization for people who are ill instead of subsidizing inoculations. With the cost of the disease reduced, the individual will be less inclined to become inoculated against the disease and hence is more likely to catch the disease and pass it on. Thus, the result of what is probably a sizable governmental expenditure in the form of a subsidy is actually an increase in the externality.

Once again, the problem is not that governmental action is not called for but that the action chosen has been badly calculated. It is quite possible for a government aiming at reducing an externality to worsen matters, but the fact that the government can make errors in this area is nothing remarkable. Governments, like other organizations, make many errors. The only moral that can be drawn from the possibility of errors is that we should be careful; we should do more research into externalities, and be very careful in applying what we already know. This is the kind of standard advice that is offered in every field and is always sensible, but has nothing specific to do with externalities.

It might be noted, however, that one aspect of this advice can be said to have an indirect bearing on the externality problem. Research, including research into externalities, is an externality-generating activity by itself. If I increase the amount of knowledge that exists in the world, it is probable that many people will benefit in addition to myself; I am creating a favorable externality. Thus, externality economics teaches us that it is desirable to stimulate further research into externality economics. Since patents are not available in this area, a system of lump sum prizes to encourage research might be sensible.

Thus far, I have confined myself fairly closely to what

might be called a standard discussion of the economics of externality, and I have avoided the voluminous literature dealing with special problems. Covering all of the many difficult, complicated details would require a much longer book. Furthermore, it seems to me that, except for people who propose to become specialists in this particular branch of economics, a detailed knowledge of these complications is not necessary. Thus, I do not intend to comprehensively cover all of the problems that have been raised in this new and really quite difficult field of economics. Nevertheless, it does seem sensible to outline some of the more important of these special problems. The first is not regarded as an externality by all economists. I do not wish to quarrel about words and, therefore, if my reader prefers not to regard the problem I am about to discuss as an example of an externality but as an example of something else, this is perfectly all right with me. It is, however, something that should be kept in mind when considering social policy.

If the government decides to spend money on anything, including an activity that might reduce an externality, it must first obtain that money. Economists long ago noted that when the government obtains money through a tax, unless the tax is the little-used head tax, there will be a burden imposed upon the society in addition to the cost of the tax itself. This so-called excess burden comes from the fact that the members of the society will not only pay their tax but they will adjust their behavior to some extent in order to reduce their tax burden. There is some cost to society imposed by this adjustment process as well as by the tax, so the net cost of the tax to the taxpayer is somewhat greater than the amount that the government collects. Thus, if the government is considering reducing an externality by a subsidy, it must first make careful calculations in which the cost of the excess burden is included. This, again, is merely a warning to be careful.

There is, however, another conclusion that can be drawn from the reasoning just given. Suppose the government is able to reduce an externality-generating activity by taxing it. Under these circumstances, the tax modifies behavior in the desired direction and at the same time provides revenue that can be used to pay for another government service. This means that the government can abandon another tax and hence that there is a gain as a result of the elimination of the excess burden of this tax.[9] If there is a choice between a tax and a subsidy, one would normally choose the tax.

Perfect adjustment frequently requires both a tax and a subsidy. Since we can hardly expect perfect adjustment, granted the imperfections of the governmental decision processes, this does not seem to be a matter of much importance. Some deviation from the optimum will occur, but it is likely to be small compared to the deviation from the optimum found in any event. Furthermore, the elimination of the excess burden on what would otherwise be taxed might well be much larger than the benefit from the subsidy.

This proposition is a partial modification of the existing orthodoxy. It has been demonstrated by Ronald Coase that it makes no difference to the ultimate outcome whether a subsidy is paid or a tax is levied.[10] The different effect on the revenue obtained by the government, however, is a relevant, if not the only consideration.

[9] See Gordon Tullock, "Excess Benefit," *Water Resources Research*, 2nd Quarter (1967), 643–644.
[10] Ronald Coase, "The Problem of Social Costs," *Journal of Law and Economics*, 3 (1960): 1–44. See also Kamien, Schwartz, and Dolbear, *Water Resources Research*, pp. 147–157, and Tullock, *Water Resources Research*, pp. 854–855.

Another and more conventional problem in connection with externality is the problem of "Pareto relevance" introduced by Buchanan and Stubblebine.[11] Suppose that my neighbor builds a house that offends me. I would be willing to pay as much as $500 to him if he would paint it another color. He, on the other hand, is quite happy with the present color and would not be willing to change it for less than $2,000. Here we clearly have a significant externality. I am suffering sizable externality costs. Nevertheless, the arrangement under which the color remains unchanged is optimal. If my preferences were much stronger, and his much weaker; if I were willing to pay $2,000 to have it repainted, and he would be willing to change it for $500, then the situation would not be Pareto optimal, but presumably we could reach an agreement.[12]

A large number of externalities are of this sort. An individual is undertaking an activity that causes pain to others or fails to provide a positive gain that other people could otherwise obtain, but the satisfaction he receives from the activity is greater than the injury or lack of gain to other people. In such cases nothing should be done. Mishan in *The Costs of Economic Growth* points out that there may be an income distribution effect.[13] Suppose I build a house on the top of a hill, and someone then buys the plot down the hill from me and proposes to build a house on it that is tall enough so that it will cut off my view. I find this objectionable. If I am wealthy, it is rather likely that I will

[11] "Externality," *Economica* (1962), p. 371, reprinted in *Readings in Welfare Economics*, ed. Kenneth J. Arrow and Tibor Scitovsky (Homewood, Ill.: Richard D. Irwin, 1969), p. 199.

[12] Note, however, the bargaining problem first introduced in the case of the rosebushes. It might or might not be an obstacle to adjustment in this case.

[13] Edward Mishan, *The Costs of Economic Growth* (New York: Frederick A. Praeger, Inc., 1967).

place a higher cash value on the damage to my view than I would if I were poor. Similarly, if the man who buys the property is wealthy, he is apt to place a higher cash value on abandoning his plan for a tall house. Thus, the outcome to some extent is determined by the relative wealth of the two parties.

This is no criticism of the normal method of computing the gain from eliminating externalities. If we approve of the current distribution of wealth in society, we are not concerned that the wealthy man is able to consume more than the poor man. There seems no reason why this should not apply to views and tall houses. If, on the other hand, we are not happy with the present distribution of wealth in society, we should do something about it directly. Once we have obtained a distribution that meets our requirements, we should not concern ourselves as to the particular ways in which people spend their money.

Another minor problem might be called the inertia effect. Considering the situation in which my neighbor is proposing to build a house that might damage my view, the amount that I would be willing to pay him to prevent his taking action after he has decided to build the house would not be enough to restrain him. However, before he had made any decision on the matter, the same payment might have led him to agree to not even plan a tall building. One can elaborate this into a problem in which it makes a difference who is to pay whom. Thus, my neighbor plans to do something that will inconvenience me in some way. I might be willing to pay him $500 not to do it, whereas the minimum amount for which he would be willing to give up his rights was $600. On the other hand, if the legal situation were such that I had an original legal right to prevent him from doing it, it might well be that he would not be willing to pay me more than (let us say) $450 for my giving up the right, while I might demand $550. This type of inertia might exist in some transactions, but I doubt that it would be common. In any event, it is difficult to see the difference. If this inertia exists, then the outcome would still be Pareto optimal, although it would, of course, be different than if there were no inertia.

A final special case of something that can be treated like an externality (although we need not call it that) is a natural monopoly. A natural monopoly is an industry with decreasing cost; that is, a larger enterprise will be able to charge lower prices than a smaller enterprise even though perhaps it earns larger profits. Under these circumstances, a free market will lead to the expansion of some enterprises and the extinction of others until either the cost of additional production by each enterprise begins to rise or until the entire market is supplied by one company. There is a great deal of debate as to whether there are many genuine examples of such industries. If we find such a situation, however, competition is impossible in the long run. Under these circumstances, it is possible for government action to improve the functioning of the economy. Unfortunately, we must emphasize it is only possible. Our experience with agencies such as the Interstate Commerce Commission would seem to indicate that government intervention will normally worsen the economy.

This experience, however, may once again simply indicate that we should improve the efficiency of the government. Government operation of a natural monopoly will perhaps not benefit the economy. It is extremely difficult to tell whether an enterprise with declining costs is actually operating efficiently or not. If the enterprise is under instructions from its owners, that is, the state, not to extort the maximum monopoly profit that can be obtained, that becomes almost impossible. The same problem exists in the case of a regulated monopoly except that in this situation we can predict with a great deal of certainty that the company will not operate efficiently and will, in fact, have much higher costs than is desirable. Still, our bad experience may indicate inept management rather than anything inherent in the nature of things.

Note, however, that if we begin looking for examples a natural monopoly, we find only a few. If we are in a country that has a high tariff barrier protecting a particular industry, it may well be that that industry is a natural monopoly in that country. Under these circumstances, a repeal of the tariff, rather than government operation, would be the proper remedy. Most other cases are situations in which, for one reason or another, it is inconvenient for several companies to operate in the same area. Electric power production is perhaps the commonest example of this situation, although it is by no means obvious that it would be impossible to have competitive distribution of power.[14] In these cases, and there are many others that may be cited, there is always a question of whether it is

[14] In the wholesale market, electricity is in fact purchased and sold in a competitive manner in the United States. The monopolies are in the retail distribution of the electricity. We will discuss the possibility of having very small governmental units covering only one or two city blocks. Such a governmental unit that took the trouble to buy its own wiring system and basic transformer (a very modest investment) could presumably purchase its electricity competitively or perhaps could even install a small diesel set. At the moment it is illegal to even experiment with this kind of thing or any other competition in provision of electricity. Here we have a case in which the laws compel a legal monopoly today, but the laws are justified by the argument that it is a natural monopoly. If it is a natural monopoly, it is hard to see why repeal of the laws would be in any way undesirable. If it is not a natural monopoly, the repeal of the laws would reveal that fact. Here we have an opportunity for social experimentation. The reader interested in further discussion of the matter should read Harold Demsetz' "Why Regulate Utilities?" *Journal of Law and Economics*, p. 55.

indeed inconvenient for several units to operate in one area. Some economists have argued that such things as milk provision and the collection of refuse are natural monopolies. If this were so, then one would anticipate that in any area in which the government does not provide these services, only one private company would operate. This is not, however, what actually occurs. Apparently the costs of having several milk wagons operate on a given street is in fact quite modest.

Note, however, that this particular natural monopoly problem is really quite similar to that of the public good. We have an activity that can be most effectively provided (if the natural monopoly argument is true) for a given region by one particular enterprise. The problem is one of contiguity. The benefits of mass production are obtained without much difficulty by General Motors, a monster organization in a fairly competitive market. In electricity provision, police services, and possibly fire prevention there are economies of scale that can be obtained in production, and it is believed that efficiency requires that contiguous areas be served by the same source of supply.[15]

As an example, in most communities of the United States there are a number of taxi companies and, although subject to price regulation by the city, they are highly competitive. In Los Angeles, however, the city council, in its wisdom, has given each of the taxi companies a monopoly on originating trips in a particular area. This has created a situation in which vast inefficiency exists but clearly the motive was to increase efficiency, producing a more efficient way of

[15] Fire prevention originally started in the United States with a number of competing fire engines paid for essentially by insurance companies. It is by no means obvious that the change to the present system benefits anyone except the insurance companies, who no longer have to support the system directly.

allocating taxies. The fact remains, however, that an artificial contiguity was created. Any individual customer is compelled to deal with a given taxi company, and yet the Los Angeles city government cannot understand why rates are high and the service is poor. Obviously, here is a case in which contiguity was produced by an unwise law and has greatly reduced the efficiency of the economy. Unfortunately, there are many cases in which the contiguity is not artificial but is a part of the nature of things.

It will be noticed that in all of the examples given, the externality is, in essence, a characteristic of the technology. One can imagine changes in technology that would eliminate the externality. Thus, as we have already noted, any statement as to what the government should or should not do is merely a statement about the present. Changes in the way we do things and improvements in technology of all sorts may well mean that the government should discontinue something it is now doing or begin doing something it is not. The old simple certainties under which one could produce a list of activities that were suitable for governmental activity have ended. The economics of externality are undeniably a scientific advance, but equally undeniably they are going to make life rather more uncertain.

# ( 5 )

# The Costs
# of Government

In this chapter we shall list the various costs of governmental action. We must begin by again emphasizing that the fact that there are costs attached to government is not a criticism of government. If we could improve the functioning of government, of course, we would greatly increase the number of functions allocated to it. Nevertheless, if we are to determine whether a given activity should be entrusted to the market, to governmental control, or to some combination of the two, we must have some idea of the costs and benefits associated with each of these institutions. We have already dealt with externalities, or the costs of the market, and now we will discuss the costs that governmental action may impose in order to learn the other part of the equation.

If we consider externalities, we find that they are large in some areas and small in others, although there are practically no areas in which they are zero. The same is true of costs of government. They are large sometimes and small elsewhere, and practically are never zero. I should like, however, to express a personal opinion that the reader may think is mere prejudice. In my opinion, many of the costs now associated with governmental action simply reflect poor design. It is my opinion that the largest single area for reform in our present society is the government itself, particularly the federal government. If we wish to improve our well-being, raise our standard of living, and improve the "quality of life," our first priority should be a drastic reform of government. Large improvements can be made in this area with correspondingly large benefits.

But this is the subject of other research and other books; let us now turn to the costs that government may impose upon individuals. Strictly speaking, we should use the Paretian apparatus. We could inquire whether those who would benefit from transferring some activity to the governmental sphere would be able to compensate those who were injured, or vice versa. This is, of course, the correct rule assuming that we are not, at the moment, talking about income distribution. Most economists would accept the results as being decisive. In this chapter, however, we will not perform this computation but simply discuss the government cost side. Later when we apply our line of reasoning to specific areas, we will consider whether compensation would be possible for transfers from the private to the public sector. It should be noted that, in general, we will be able to make only qualitative judgments. The empirical data are not yet available for a definitive answer to most of these problems.

Turning, then, to the costs of government; the first such cost is one we have already discussed, the fact that the governmental decision will characteristically not be the optimum decision for any given voter. The individual voter must make an estimate as to what the governmental decision is likely to be and thus decide from his standpoint whether governmental activity is better or worse than private activity. It is clear, however, that there will be a great many voters for whom the governmental decision will be nonoptimal and for these voters, there is a cost (even though the cost may well be less than the cost generated by externalities in the private market). In Figure 9, on the horizontal axis (which is all there is to this figure) is shown the amount of a typical governmental activity that could be undertaken. Let us begin by assuming that a simple majority vote is held to determine the desired amount of activity by the government. If we assume that the voters are randomly distributed along the continuum and that their preference intensities are either equal or randomly distributed, then a simple majority voting process will reach the same point as would be reached if the parties were permitted to bargain for an infinite period of time and finally decide after side-payments how much the government would do.[1]

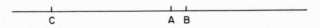

C          A   B

FIGURE 9. Quantity of a Governmental Activity

In other words, under these circumstances simple majority voting will achieve a solution that is equivalent to the Paretian process except for distribution. An individual would have some costs as a result of the fact that his preference is not the majority voting outcome, point A. In practice, of course, he will not be compensated for the

[1] In the next few pages a number of conclusions about the political process will be presented that are based on reasoning contained in James Buchanan and Gordon Tullock, *The Calculus of Consent* (Ann Arbor: University of Michigan Press, 1962).

reasons we discussed in Chapter 1. If we permitted people not only to vote on the exact amount of the government provision but also to seek compensation, we would face an impossible bargaining problem. Hence the individual faces a straightforward uncompensated loss as a result of the governmental action. It is, of course, only inappropriate from his standpoint, rather than from the standpoint of the total group, but theoretically one can compute the average cost that individuals would suffer. In order to make such computations, we would have to make some assumptions of the distribution of the people and the amount to which they are injured by the lack of optimality in the quantity of goods purchased. Instead of making these computations, which would be of little use to us unless they were based upon empirical knowledge that we do not have, let us inquire as to the change in these costs from varying political arrangements.

First, suppose we simply divided the population affected by this governmental activity into two randomly selected samples. What effect would this have? Presumably, if these two samples are large, the midpoints of their distributions, and therefore, the points they would choose by majority voting, would be very close together and very close to point A on our diagram. Nevertheless, they would not be identical. Furthermore, the sample whose optima lay to the right of point A would have more people in it whose optima lay to the right, and the sample whose optima lay to the left of point A would have more people whose optima lay to the left. The result of this would be that the average distance of the individuals from the collective decision controlling them would be reduced. Probably with larger samples, this would be a tiny effect, but continuing the subdividing we would get small samples. These small samples would have considerable variance, and this effect would become quite significant. Ultimately, of course, we would have one person in each area and in that event, there would be perfect adjustment.[2] All of this is, once again, to make the point made in the first chapter. In general, the larger the governmental unit the less likely it is that any individual will have his preferences perfectly satisfied. This factor must, of course, be set off against the externality that may be best dealt with by a fairly large governmental unit.

We do not, however, have to select our sample in a random way. Suppose, for example, there were some way of pulling out a sample of about 20 per cent that was heavily skewed toward the left end. If we did this, we would then be able to have two collective decision processes producing two different outcomes, one shown at point C, and another shown at point B. This would materially improve the satisfaction of the parties and government cost would be less.

The obvious example, of course, is the use of geographically limited local governments. Characteristically, each small area is indeed somewhat different in its needs from other small areas and hence the division of the government into small jurisdictions is desirable,[3] insofar as it can be done without raising significant externality problems. We need not, however, confine ourselves to this particular method of dividing government. It may be possible to cut out some functional activity rather than cutting out a geographical area. The average private club is an example of this since it provides some type of public good that its

[2] Cf. Yoram Barzel, "Two Propositions on the Optimum Level of Producing Collective Goods," *Public Choice*, 6 (Spring 1969): 31–37.

[3] Cf. Vincent Ostrom, "Operational Federalism: Organization for the Provision of Public Services in the American Federal System," *Public Choice*, 6 (Spring 1969): 1–17, and Gordon Tullock, "Federalism: Problems of Scale," *Public Choice*, 6 (Spring 1969): 19–29.

members value more than does society in general. Whether this public good is a golf course, flying field, or simply an opportunity for discussion, the fact remains that there is an improvement in the organization of society as a result of the existence of this particular private organization. There are a great many similar specialized boards which control various types of activities. Normally these are, in fact, controlled by the participants in the activity. Unfortunately, in the real world these boards are often mainly concerned with strengthening the cartel power of their members.

Another possible example that has occurred to me would be a special governmental agency to control highways.[4] In the United States, the highways are largely self-supporting, being paid for by gasoline taxes. Thus an arrangement under which the decisions as to the use of highways, construction of new highways, and highway regulations were determined by a special elective body in which only (let us say) automobile owners were permitted to vote might produce an improved allocation of resources, although, of course, it may not. Still, it seems an idea worthy of further consideration.

Note that it is possible only because both the taxes and the benefits accrue to the same people. If we permitted one small group of people to decide how much was to be spent in a given area, but collected the taxes from the population at large, we would then be creating a governmental externality. Unfortunately, such things are also quite common in the present world. They are intriguing because they are almost perfect examples of private externalities although they exist in the governmental sphere. Their further discussion must, however, be deferred.

---

[4] This would not necessarily be a single national organization; a number of local organizations would be possible.

If we examine the type of acts that are passed by Congress or the administrative decisions made by governments, we observe that most of them do not deal with matters that concern the whole population. Characteristically, they involve the expenditure of government funds for the benefit of a fairly small part of the population. Note that this is not said in a critical spirit. Of necessity, the decision to build a road network will be composed of a large number of individual decisions to build each part of it. Each one of these partial decisions to build or to improve a short length of road will primarily benefit only a small portion of the population. Nevertheless, the population as a whole has a real interest in the existence of the entire road network. The same can be said for a large number of other governmental activities.

It must, of course, be admitted that there are a considerable number in any government's list of activities that should never be undertaken. Tulsa, Oklahoma, is now advertising itself as the world's newest port. Unfortunately, this claim is perfectly true. A group of adroit congressmen have succeeded in maneuvering the federal government into dredging a nine-foot channel to Tulsa. Clearly, this is an activity whose benefits are confined to an *extremely* small group of people.

But let us confine ourselves to activities that it is reasonably clear that the government should undertake (such as road repair and extension of the road network). In Figure 10 the preferences of the population are shown with respect to a particular road repair project. Since this road by definition directly serves only a limited area, the bulk of the population has little interest in its being repaired and is aware of the fact that they will pay in taxes for the repair. Their interest, then, is to keep the road in an eco-

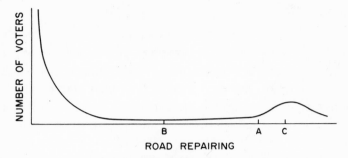

FIGURE 10. Distribution of Optima with Respect to the Quantity of Some Governmental Activity

nomical state of disrepair. They are aware of the fact that the economy of the country is to some extent affected by this road, but they feel, quite correctly, that the effect on them is very small compared to the tax cost. The people who live on the road, on the other hand (who will, after all, pay only a small part of the cost of repairing it if it is repaired out of general funds), in general would like to have it repaired, and their preferences are shown at the far right of the diagram in the small hump. If this matter is put to a simple majority vote, we would end up at point B or somewhere to its left. In this case, however, this is not a Pareto optimal decision. The people who have a desire to have the road repaired could, most assuredly, compensate the others for the movement to the right. The reason for this is that their interest in the road repair is much more intense than is the interest of the remainder of the voters in the rather small increase in their taxes. The result of computing what would be the optimal bargaining would be some point such as point A on the continuum.

If we have logrolling, or if we have a central government that makes up programs in general that have the effect of implicit logrolling, then it is likely that the road will be

103

repaired; hence, the institution of logrolling does improve the general satisfaction of the community. Unfortunately, if we have simple majority voting, the amount of repair work put in on the road under these circumstances would be considerably greater than the optimal outcome, the amount C in fact. Under these circumstances, simple majority voting, if taken on each individual issue, leads to point B that probably is hardly (if at all) better than market provision of road services, and logrolling leads to C, which is clearly very much better than market provision.[5] Under either of these assumptions, majority voting does not work as well as it does where the voters are relatively evenly distributed both in intensity and in location along the issue dimension.

Here we have an area in which we could hope for institutional reform. If the number of votes required to cause the road to be repaired is raised from a simple majority to a somewhat higher number, let us say two-thirds, the logrolling process will continue to work, but the eventual outcome will be moved closer to point A, which is the Pareto optimal outcome. Thus the cost to the individual as a result of placing this particular activity under government control would be less under qualified majority rule. Furthermore, this would mean that various governmental activities, which would be best to leave in private hands under simple majority voting, would be suitable objects for collectivization if we were using something like a two-thirds or three-quarters voting rule. The increase in the required majority by reducing the costs of collective provision of the activity in question would make the collective provision more

[5] The reasoning upon which this conclusion and those immediately following are based may be found in Buchanan and Tullock, *The Calculus of Consent*.

efficient and hence in these cases would make it desirable to switch from private provision.

In situations such as those shown on Figure 10, there may, however, be another and indeed superior available procedure. Governments have, like Topsy, just grown, but radical institutional revision may still be possible. As a first approximation, let us assume that the tax structure is changed so that when a road is repaired the entire cost of repairing that road falls on the people who live close to it. Under these circumstances, we could set up a separate constituency to vote on the tax and road repair project alone, and they would make their choice considering that all the cost falls upon themselves. This would lead them to want less road repairing than if they can induce someone else to pay the bulk of the cost, and we could use simple majority voting, perhaps, to achieve the optimal result. The problems are obvious, such as the problem of actually defining the area that is to vote, the fact that road repairing and road extension projects are not really continuous over large areas. It is notable that in many parts of the United States at any event, small local government districts with jurisdiction only over certain specialized problems (mosquito abatement is one) have been established. Whether they are the right size and, therefore, produce the most efficient output is something on which I cannot offer any judgment. Here, again, research is needed.

But most economists reading the above paragraph would immediately object that it is not just the people who live right near a given road who have an interest in having it repaired. The voters at the left end of the spectrum want some money spent on the repair of the road, and are aware of the fact that the road network as a whole benefits them. There is again a simple procedure that is available. Let us suppose that the central government under the control of the mass of voters simply subsidizes the local road repair projects. It offers, let us say, to pay half the cost and then permits the local governmental agencies to choose which roads they will repair and how much they will spend. This clearly is a case in which we are using the standard Pigouvian method of subsidy to deal with an externality. This method is widely used. The federal government, for example, is obtaining the construction of an interstate highway system by paying 90 per cent of the cost, but many of the decisions as to where the highway will be built are left to the local authorities who put up the other 10 per cent.

The last example indicates the danger of this type of arrangement. It is fairly clear that the 90 per cent of the cost is vastly in excess of the amount that should be offered for the improvement of roads in a restricted area. Here we have a case in which a mechanism that theoretically seems sensible has been used in such a way that it probably causes substantial diseconomies.[6] The fact, however, does not mean that correct calculations to prevent this result are impossible. The problem is that it is, at present, impossible to design a voting procedure that would produce the correct division between state, central, and local governments.

This discussion of logrolling may impress the reader as not being realistic. We do not often observe individual voters engaging in logrolling—that is done mainly by the representatives in the legislature. We observe direct logrolling only in rare town meetings. There is, of course, something similar to logrolling in party platforms.[7] This

[6] These diseconomies are not as great as you might think, because as a matter of fact the federal government sometimes refuses to provide the money. Granted the situation in which the federal government has put itself by adopting a 90 per cent subsidy, this is very wise.

[7] See my *Entrepreneurial Politics*, Thomas Jefferson Center Monograph #5, University of Virginia.

criticism is both correct and slightly misleading. We can consider how the government would work if the individual voter had more direct control over it. The fact that he does not have this degree of control over what the government does surely results in a reduction of his satisfaction. If we observe an individual purchasing things in the market, we see that he is able to make direct decisions on a great number of different issues. His decision whether to buy apples or oranges and the quantity of each is made several times a week during the course of a year. In the course of the average year, the individual makes something on the order of 15,000 to 20,000 buying decisions. If we turn to the political sphere, however, we find that the individual characteristically makes very few decisions. Surely this must lead to inefficiency in governmental maximization of his utility function.

We can imagine a situation in which an individual entered into a contract with a department store, with the store agreeing to provide the individual with all his needs for a year in return for some initial price—this contract to be renewable from year to year but not changeable during the year. Clearly, this would greatly reduce the individual's satisfaction. This is more or less what we do in government. The individual must choose between two monstrous packages of services every time he votes instead of choosing in an incremental manner from a large number of small packages as he does in the market. The inefficiency is clear, and unfortunately it is not very obvious that a great deal can be done about it, although the situation is more the result of historical accident than of careful design.

There seem to be three basic reasons why we make rather few political choices through the voting process in contrast to the number of economic choices we make in the market. The first of these is simply an obsolete political theory. The second is the fact that voting has traditionally been generally more of a bothersome procedure than purchasing, and hence, people have economized on the number of votes they will cast; and the third is that the information problems that occur in voting are not as severe in the market.

The founding fathers were at one with the rest of the world in believing in a theory of politics that can best be described as aristocratic. It has often been said that they based their work on Montesquieu's misunderstanding of the British Constitution. The theory, however, dates back to Aristotle. In this view, individuals select the best people from the community who then go to a central place and form the government. The individual is not thought of as registering direct preferences on government action, but only as selecting a superior individual who will participate in the government. Under this theory, frequent or detailed elections would not be required. In its pure form, this theory is no longer held by anyone, but in discussing political matters with traditional students of political science, or indeed with most people who have thought about this matter and become accustomed to traditional literature, I have always found they still retain elements of "The Old Belief." To them government is not, like the market, simply a mechanism to obtain our preferences, insofar as possible; it has some higher goal.

I must say that in my discussions with these people I have never been able to find out exactly what this higher goal is.[8] Furthermore, these people themselves recognize differences of opinion as to what these higher goals should be. Never-

---

[8] Those who are of religious inclination are sometimes able to specify higher goals in terms of whatever particular religion they happen to believe in.

theless, it *is* clear that simply satisfying the individual is not the objective they have in mind. The government is supposed to do things that are good for the individual, not things that the individual wants. Now if we assume that somehow or other governments do have information on what is "good for" the individual, and that they act on it, then the individual himself would find that his preferences are not maximized in the short run, although in the long run they might be. He would have to make a decision as to whether he wanted whatever he wanted now, or whether he proposed to submit to the judgment of someone else who might give a better long run level of satisfaction.[9]

If the individual is not convinced that these people actually know more about what will please him than he does himself, then clearly he will suffer a cost from a government that is organized, not to give him what he wants, but to give him what someone thinks he "should" want. The exact size of this cost would depend on the difference between the individual's preference function and the objectives of the government. There is little that can be said in general except that there is surely no reason to believe that a government that is not attempting to maximize individual satisfaction will, in fact, do so as a by-product. It would seem on the whole that an individual given his choice between market activity and governmental activity would wish to submit relatively little of his life to governmental activity if the government is not, even theoretically, functioning as an apparatus for carrying out individual desires in some aggregative form.

[9] Here, again, there is some oversimplification. Many of these people apparently do not really think that what is good for people is what gives them satisfaction even in the long run. Some sort of higher goal, higher, that is, than the happiness of the people, is apparently somewhat cloudily present.

In practice, of course, democratic governments are not attempting to impose higher values.[10] In practice, politicians are the people we elect to office in a democracy, and normally, as part of their campaign, they make promises as to what policies they will carry out. Furthermore, once they are elected, they normally want to be reelected, and hence in choosing their policies, politicians pay careful attention to the preferences of the voters. As we shall see, information problems may lead them to do things that the bulk of the voters may dislike. Their intention, however, is not to impose some higher values on the voter, but to get reelected.

The theory that government should not maximize individual preferences or should not try to act as a preference aggregating system can be described as a normative theory. One can say that this is what one would like the government to do, but one cannot say that this is what the governments in democracies actually do. Governments in democracies characteristically are attempting to do things that they think will get them reelected and this means that they must pay careful attention to the preference functions of their citizens. Thus, the individual who wants his preference maximized can feel fairly confident that if some activity is transferred from the private sphere to the government sphere, the government will not simply try to impose its own preference. The government will be engaged in an effort to determine what will gain the most votes and will count his vote among those it wishes to gain. This may not in all cases be of much help to him, but it is better than a government that is trying to reach some goal different from that of the voter.

---

[10] Nondemocratic governments may very well be engaged in this. It must be remembered that only a few of the people who have lived in the world have lived under democracies.

The previous line of reasoning, I suspect, will strike most economists as being simple and obvious, and they will wonder why I have spent so much time on it. The political scientist, on the other hand, will probably feel that what I am saying is absurd. My last academic appointment was a joint one at both the Political Science and Economics departments at Rice University. I found a complete difference in attitude in my colleagues in these two areas. The political scientists always assured me that I was wrong—that the point of government was not simply to do what the people want. In fact, they thought this would be an inferior objective of government. I was, however, unable to discover exactly what the government was supposed to do, if this was not its objective. "The integrative function" or the "authoritative allocation of values" seem to be slogans with little content, but I may just not be understanding them. At any event, I am compelled to proceed on my present state of information, although I must admit it may be imperfect in this respect.

But if the people who design most modern governments did not operate on the theory that the government was attempting to maximize individual preferences, this is not a reason for not using this theory. If we do follow it, we should consider the possibility of increasing the number of occasions on which individuals are enabled to affect the political order in the direction of their preferences. Our system of competing department stores that provided goods on a yearly contract to everyone would clearly be improved if the contract were shortened to six months or, for that matter, if smaller stores handling rather different lines of business were created and if each individual was permitted to enter into contracts with more than one store. Eventually, of course, if we kept breaking the contracts up into smaller and smaller units, we would reach our present market arrangement. There seems to be no reason why we could not similarly reduce the choice unit in politics, although the information problems, which are to be discussed shortly, place stringent limitations on the amount of such division that can be undertaken in politics.

Before discussing the possibility of having individuals more frequently express their preferences through the vote, perhaps as frequently as in Switzerland, the mechanical problems of voting should be mentioned. The standard method of voting that we have inherited from our ancestors involves the individual's going to a location designated by the authorities, which is frequently not conveniently located and seldom within a few feet of his home or business, and there expressing his opinion by casting a vote. The entire procedure is fairly time consuming. Furthermore, the government itself is put to a considerable expense in maintaining the election machinery. There is no one, as there is in the private market, who has a positive material motive to make the choice process easier or more convenient, and hence we do not have the convenience of transaction that exists in the commercial market. Under modern circumstances, or to be more exact, under the circumstances that will occur in a year or so, this degree of inconvenience is clearly unnecessary. There is no intrinsic reason why the telephone system and computers could not be linked to permit anyone who wished to vote to do so in his own home or place of business.

James C. Miller has worked out a system under which individuals could exercise a great degree of direct supervision over government by casting direct votes, or alternatively if they wished, could designate representatives in the legislature to vote for them. At the moment the system would be rather expensive but if the electronics industry continues to progress, it should become fairly inexpensive in the next five to ten years.[11] Thus, the physical inconvenience of present-day voting is unnecessary. It could be made inexpensive for the voter, and the voting apparatus itself, now a complex and inefficient set of election judges and guards, could be replaced by a computer. With the costs of voting reduced, the voting process could obviously be used to greater advantage. Clearly, in this situation purely mechanical governmental reform is desirable. The present degree of aggregation of voting must lead to a lower level of satisfaction than could be obtained if the individual were given an opportunity to express his opinion in a more finely structured way. The techniques are available and they should be implemented.

Nevertheless, if we are talking about current costs of government, the individual is faced with a situation in which he has relatively little control over governmental activity simply because he votes fairly rarely. When he does vote, he normally votes on a highly aggregated bundle of issues, which must be considered when one compares the market with the government. At the moment, then, we would anticipate that individuals would choose market provision over government provision in those circumstances in which they would make the opposite choice if the voting process were reformed.

A large number of elections on a large number of issues would probably be quite a considerable trial for the voter, but in his capacity as customer in the private market, the voter is not required to make decisions on matters in which he does not wish to decide. He can simply refrain from

[11] James C. Miller, III, "A Program for Direct and Proxy Voting in the Legislative Process," *Public Choice*, 7 (Fall 1969): 49–66.

going into the store. Similarly, the existence of a large number of issues on which the voter was permitted to express his preference but not compelled to do so, might well work out the same way. The individual would choose to vote on those issues that he thought might sufficiently affect his interest so that it would be worth the effort to cast the vote and leave the others to his representative. Thus, we may have a large number of votes with relatively few people voting directly at each election. Given perfect information, there is no reason why this process would not work perfectly. As we shall see when we discuss the information limitations that actually exist in the political area, it is possible that this system would work out very badly indeed. Still, it should be remembered that every individual voter does not have to vote in every individual election and, hence, multiplying the number of elections does not necessarily produce an increase in cost for the voter.

In regard to the information problem, however, we find ourselves faced with much greater difficulties. It is possible that the information situation in politics can be improved, but it is fairly clear that voter information will always be much poorer than the information possessed by customers in the market. Unfortunately, we cannot express the exact importance of this relative ignorance. All we know is that this particular difficulty does exist in the political sphere, at least in democracies, and that it should be taken into account. It is possible that empirical research might eventually achieve a measure of this phenomenon, but at the moment we have no such data.

If we consider what empirical work has been done in this area, however, we find extraordinary evidence of ignorance in the political field. Voters who do not know the name of their congressmen are common, and ignorance of the stands taken by the parties on major issues is even more common. Furthermore, the information that people do obtain is largely a by-product of entertainment. Conversation, for example, is a major source of political information-gathering. The traditional response of students of politics to the obvious ignorance of the voters has been to lecture the voters on their duty to learn more. There is no evidence that this has had any great effect, and recently students, beginning with Anthony Downs, have realized that the individual voter has actually behaved quite rationally in not acquiring much information.[12]

The reasons for this can be easily understood if we refer to our small Iowa community of 1,000 making a decision on the level of collective mosquito abatement. The individual voter will be aware (if he is rational) of the fact that the odds are heavily against his being the median voter. If this is so, if he does not learn much about the issue and inaccurately specifies his preference in the voting process, it will have no effect on the outcome unless he makes a gigantic error and actually votes on the other side of the median from his "true position." Even in this case he will cause only a slight change in the outcome; he will move the median by one voter. If the voter suspects that he himself might be the median voter and hence that his preference would determine the outcome, an error on his part would only make a slight difference.

The voter in this case would rationally set off the cost of improving his information against the likely effect that that information will have on the outcome of the election. If the individual is considering purchasing something at a given cost, he is motivated to investigate the qualities of the

[12] Anthony Downs, *An Economic Theory of Democracy* (New York: Harper & Row Publishers, Inc., 1958).

thing he is purchasing to an extent that discounts the value of an erroneous choice to him. If he is participating in a collective decision process, however, he must further discount the value of the item by the weight of his own contribution to the decision. For further information on this subject, the reader is referred to my book *Toward a Mathematics of Politics*.[13] The outcome of the reasoning is simply that the voter will spend less resources in obtaining information on political issues than on private purchases. Furthermore, this difference can be extremely great. Lastly, this theoretical prediction is abundantly confirmed by empirical investigations.

From the economist's standpoint, however, there might appear to be a strong argument against what I have just been saying. The slogan *de gustibus non est disputandum* has been an important one for a long time, and it might appear that all that the political process should be expected to do is give the voter what he wants regardless of his state of information. Although we do not greatly concern ourselves with his state of information in the marketplace, economists have almost always felt that measures to improve information are desirable. Government acts requiring accurate labeling or requiring organizations to make certain information public have normally been supported by economists. When they have been objected to, the objections have normally taken the form of claiming not that there are no benefits, but that the costs associated with them are greater than the benefits.

Theoretically, we can see that we do concern ourselves with information in spite of the slogan *chacun à son goût* by considering the possibility of a tax on information. Sup-

[13] Gordon Tullock, *Toward a Mathematics of Politics* (Ann Arbor: University of Michigan Press, 1966), chaps. 7, 8.

pose, for example, that people were taxed a specific amount per minute of time spent obtaining information on the purchase of major items. Disregarding the difficulty of administering such a tax, I suppose that economists would agree that this tax would have a substantial excess burden. Furthermore, this excess burden must take the form of reducing the efficiency of the purchasing process, in spite of the fact that the individuals buy whatever car, radio, or other item that they want. Thus, in this case, we are interested in the quality of their expressed preferences.

This mystery, insofar as it is a mystery, is easily explained. Individuals, in fact, have preferences for different qualities of products. The investigation that they undertake in the marketplace is to help them determine whether a particular product or service will provide them with what they want. The more energy they expend in their investigations, the greater is the likelihood that the ultimate purchase will be satisfactory to them. The individual theoretically makes continuous estimates as to whether the additional satisfaction from improving his purchase by acquiring more information is equal to the cost to him of acquiring that additional information. This cost to a large extent is the delay in making the purchase. He continues to acquire information until the margins meet, and then he buys.

In the political marketplace the problem is that the amount of information that one would normally acquire is usually extremely small. If my decision on the amount that should be purchased will only have a tiny and probably insignificant effect on the amount that I do purchase through a collective procedure, it is likely that I will invest relatively little time and effort in becoming well informed. Thus, I will normally make a much poorer adjustment to

117

my basic preferences than I would in the market. People in the real world clearly behave this way. Furthermore, the political parties and candidates seem to be aware of this and plan their arguments to the voter in terms of a relatively ignorant audience. There seem to be three basic political "platforms." One is an effort by the candidate to impress people that he is indeed a nice fellow, which is probably the major single political activity of most candidates. The canvassing in England and the more elaborate campaign methods normally used in the United States where the constituencies are larger both have this as their major objective.

A second "argument" that is very widely used in most political systems is an effort to get voters who have no preference at all to vote for their candidate simply by asking them to do so. Stephen Shadegg's *How to Win an Election* is a clear and direct statement of this technique by a man who has had great experience in organizing elections.[14] The issues are also discussed by the candidates because there are various people who are interested in specific issues. Normally, however, the people who are interested in the issues are only interested in one or two issues that directly concern them. The minority of the populace who are interested in all of the issues, the intellectuals, are not only a minority but as far as we can see they do not significantly change their position from election to election and hence are not likely to be affected by a discussion of the issues. Once again, I have discussed these matters in greater detail in *Toward a Mathematics of Politics*.[15]

The costs inflicted upon us by this relatively poor infor-

[14] Stephen C. Shadegg, *How to Win an Election* (New York: Taplinger Publishing Co., 1964).
[15] Gordon Tullock, *Toward a Mathematics of Politics*, chaps. 7, 8.

mation in the political process must be great. We can now turn to the question of what can be done about it. There seem to be several possibilities. Preaching has been widely tried by political scientists and has had little effect. A second possibility would be an effort to introduce fair labeling laws into the political area of the type now in effect in the commercial area. The problems connected with these laws are extreme—they are not so much technical problems in the pure sense as they are problems that are raised by the fact that the politicians themselves would, of necessity, enforce these laws. One would worry about the prospect of the party in power using these laws to damage its opponents.[16] Nevertheless, it seems that there should be some experimentation carried out along these lines. Individuals are not totally uninterested in obtaining information on political matters; they just have a very slight interest. Under these circumstances, compelling people to provide information may have much more effect than it would have in the market. But this is merely a suggestion; I cannot be sure that it would be of any great use. In any event, it is a palliative and does not cure the problem as a whole.

Another prospect would be to eliminate the present strong social pressure to vote. It is likely that if these pressures were reduced, the total number of people voting would decline, and the people who stopped voting would, on the whole, be the less informed. I do not know how much this would improve the situation, but it surely should have at least some helpful effect. The person who voluntarily chose not to invest his resources in going to the polls would also likely be the person who had chosen not to

[16] Treason doth never prosper; what's the reason?
Why if it prosper, none dare call it treason.
Sir John Harington, *Epigrams, of Treason*

invest resources in becoming informed. Thus our rather elaborate indoctrination in the schools and the public opinion molding activities at election periods for the purpose of getting out the vote are probably counterproductive.

As mentioned before, the fact that the voter is badly informed means that the optimum detail in voting choices is not likely to involve as much differentiation as that observed in market choice. It still seems likely, however, that at least some additional differentiation would be desirable. Furthermore, it might make the information problem easier for the voter. It may be easier to make up one's mind on ten different votes, each of which governs 10 per cent of government activity, than it is to make a decision on only a single vote that covers the entire scope of governmental activity. Lastly, if the division of the activity covered by the individual elections involved more use of local governmental agencies, then the voter actually has a net reduction in his total decision load. If highways are decided upon by a national agency upon which we vote, then each individual must decide how many highways are to be built all over the United States. If, on the other hand, highway expenditures are chosen locally, he will make decisions only about the local highways. Surely the latter is likely to be a more informed decision. This factor would, as is usual when we talk of the cost of government, have to be laid off against the externalities that could be brought under control if we had a national or indeed world government building our highways.

There is one way in which one can conceive of government services being provided where the individual voter-customer would have the same incentives to obtain information as he does in the market. Americans move a great deal; the average family moves from one city to another every five years. Characteristically this move will involve, among other things, a consideration of the governmental services that are obtainable in the various localities. In fact, in the area surrounding large cities, movements from one area to another are not infrequently caused by differences in governmental services. Superior schools, in particular, are likely to attract families to a given suburb.

Clearly, the individual in "purchasing" government by deciding where to live is in much the same position as the individual who is buying a car. His decision is controlling, and hence, he is motivated to obtain information. Thus, if we could somehow arrange a competitive market in governments, we would anticipate that the information problems we have been discussing would be greatly reduced. Something of this sort actually does exist in the United States, and I suspect, in other countries. Unfortunately, for a variety of reasons, it is not very well developed and is probably doomed to remain permanently relatively undeveloped.

There are two aspects to the "competitive provision of government." The first is private provision of a limited collection of "governmental" services. There are now a number of private enterprises that establish communities in which a great many potential externalities have been internalized by the management. Characteristically, they do not provide the total scope of governmental services and thus do not produce totally competitive governments. It is an interesting, but as far as I know, completely unexplored, question as to whether or not one might extend this idea so that private corporations provided the total of governmental services for some particular area. The dangers are obvious, but it is not by any means certain that they could not be overcome. In any event, at the moment these organizations (which will be discussed in more detail later) are a relatively minor and modest feature of the political landscape. Normally, they provide only a small part of the services that would ordinarily be provided by government.

The second area in which governmental competition exists is the previously mentioned suburban area surrounding a large city, where a large number of communities may be found in which individuals make choices among these communities. The reason that this competitive market in governmental services does not function like a private competitive market is that the individual "enterprises" are not run by profit maximizing entrepreneurs. Once an individual moves into a community he becomes a voter, and the voters in the communities behave very much like voters elsewhere. Thus, although the individual makes his initial choice of the community in which he lives in much the same way as he makes his choice of a car, he is choosing among communities that are run by relatively inattentive voters. Furthermore, the motives that may lead the voters in some particular community to favor desirable political institutions in order to attract immigrants from other communities, are not very strong.

Thus, although the individual moving into a suburban community makes a choice that is as well informed as his market choices, the communities themselves are not managed by people who are vigorously attempting to increase the number of "customers" they receive. In consequence, this "market" works badly. Nevertheless, anyone who has lived in a large metropolitan area will realize that this factor (the tendency of people to move in and out of communities depending upon the line of services offered) does exert some pressure for increased efficiency. Here, again, it might be possible to reorganize government so that individual choices would be of greater importance. Unfortunately, I can offer no present ideas as to how this can be done, but it does not seem to be totally beyond the mind of man.

In most discussions of the costs of government, bureaucracy is emphasized. Complaints about bureaucracy in government are an omnipresent feature of modern life and such complaints are in general justified. Clearly, most modern governments are appallingly badly organized. If we are considering placing a particular activity under governmental control, we should, of course, take into account the fact that this means expanding an already swollen bureaucracy, and that the particular activity we are placing under governmental control will probably be handled in much the same way as the Post Office.

But it is reasonable to ask whether this cost is necessary. It is certainly true that today we have vast and inefficient bureaucracies. Is there no way of producing more efficient bureaucracies? If we could organize the government in a more efficient way, presumably we would wish to entrust more activities to it because its cost would be less. Before discussing the possibilities of improvement, we might inquire briefly why it is that General Motors, a very large organization, seems to have less difficulty with its bureaucracy than does the smaller government Post Office. First, we must note that it is not true that General Motors has absolutely no difficulty; in fact, anyone who has had contact with large corporations is aware of the fact that bureaucracy is also a real problem there. It is, however, a lesser problem. There is now a beginning of serious research into internal organization of large hierarchal structures of which any bureaucracy is an example. From this research it would appear that the difficulties that most Western nations have with their governmental bureaucracy to a very large extent simply represent poor design, whereas the type of difficulties that are faced by General Motors are, to a considerable extent, the minimum residual that can be obtained with good design. There are, however, as we shall see, certain special problems that would perhaps make governmental bureaucracy less efficient in any event.

The problem faced by any designer of a bureaucracy is that he must employ human beings to act as his bureaucrats and they have individual objectives that are not necessarily those that would be desired by the organizer of the bureaucracy. The larger the bureaucracy and the less it is possible to reduce its objectives to some single numerical measure such as profit, the more likely it is that the individual bureaucrats will be able to follow their individual preferences rather than the preferences of the "organization." Thus, reduction in size and increasingly detailed specification of what is wanted from the bureaucracy will normally help. In this connection, William Niskanen, who has had many years of experience in attempting to improve the efficiency of one particularly large bureaucracy, the Department of Defense, has suggested various methods whereby one might impose upon segments of the gigantic bureaucracy somewhat similar conditions as those faced by segments of General Motors.[17] These proposals are at the moment tentative, and I do not think anyone (certainly not Niskanen) regards them as more than suggestions for research. But they do indicate that a possibility of drastic reform in bureaucracy does exist and that, therefore, great improvements in the functioning of government might be possible. Again, such improvements would make it sensible

[17] William Niskanen, "The Peculiar Economics of Bureaucracy," *American Economic Review*, 58, no. 2 (May 1968): 293-305.

to entrust a greater portion of our society to government hands instead of to the market.

There appears, however, to be one very serious problem in connection with governmental bureaucracies as opposed to private bureaucracies, at least in a democracy. Characteristically, in a democracy, minorities who are deeply concerned with a given issue have disproportionate influence. Unfortunately, the bureaucrats themselves are such an intense minority, and they are interested in the expansion of their power and financial base. Thus, they are able to, in part, specify that one of the objectives toward which any governmental enterprise will aim is the benefiting of its employees. Indeed, in numerous cases, it would appear that benefits to the employees and to the private companies that supply the given segment of the bureaucracy are the principal "goods" generated by the organization.

This means that many programs do not really achieve very much in the way of meeting their ostensible objectives. At the time that I write this book, the United States government has for a number of years been engaging in something known as the "War on Poverty," which has involved the spending of large sums of money to allegedly help the poor. It is notable, however, that the help that the poor have actually received from these programs is really quite modest.[18] It apparently costs about $15,000 to $20,000 a year per person to set up a program that will train a poor person to occupy a job in which he might receive, after a number of years, a yearly salary of $3,000 to $4,000. The seepage into the bureaucratic morass (and, it must be admitted, into paying off local politicians) is much greater

[18] In the trade, the phenomenon is known as "feeding the sparrows by feeding the horses."

than the nominal impact of the program. Clearly, one of the major reasons for this is that the bureaucrats vote. They are an intense minority who are able to convert many bureaucracies from agencies aimed at defending the country, suppressing crime, and helping the poor into agencies whose principal output is providing amenities for bureaucrats and for whom the defense of the country, repression of crime, and aid to the poor is somewhat of a by-product.

But here again, we come up against the economist's motto, *de gustibus non est disputandum*. If what the voters want is employment for themselves, as bureaucrats, then why not? The answer to this question would appear to be that most of us would not in fact be interested in setting up a bureaucracy ostensibly for the purpose of helping the poor if its principal real effect would be merely to employ a number of bureaucrats at above the market wages, with very little help to the poor. If our choice is leaving the poor to the tender mercies of private charity, or placing it in the hands of a bureaucracy, which, in fact, will pay little attention to the poor and very much attention to its own private gain, we might well choose the private charity even if we thought the private charity was basically quite inadequate. In other words, it may be that the fact that bureaucrats are able to distort agencies into instrumentalities for supporting themselves would mean that the cost of establishing such agencies would be vastly in excess of the benefits for any but the bureaucrats.

This is speculation, however, and we cannot be sure how large the effect of this type of bureaucratic activity is. It should be noted that theoretically there is a fairly simple and straightforward remedy. We could deprive the bureaucrats, their families, government suppliers, indeed anyone who obtains a significant portion of his income from dealing with the government, of the vote. Radical as this proposal may seem, it is hard to offer any very strong argument against it. The bureaucrats are such a large part of our population that it is unlikely that their attitudes toward political matters are greatly different from those of the population as a whole, if we abstract out only their attitude toward their own bureau's expansion and their own salary. They should be simply a very large random sample. If this is so, then the only difference resulting from the abolition of the vote of bureaucrats would be that the bureaucrat's interests would not be pushed by a particular pressure group of voters.

Since the bureaucrats would obtain the full market value of their services without this type of pressure (because they cannot be hired if they are not paid as much as they can obtain elsewhere) this would not harm them unless they are now receiving more than the full value of their services. It seems difficult to argue that bureaucrats should receive more than the value of their services. Thus, it would seem to be difficult to produce any valid argument against depriving bureaucrats of the vote. Needless to say, I do not anticipate that this logical difficulty will significantly impede criticism of this portion of my book.

In this chapter, we have reviewed many distinct and fairly sizable costs of governmental action. In the previous chapter we covered externalities that made it certain that private activities in many areas would have greater costs. In every case, the problem that we face when deciding whether some activity shall be market or governmental is the minimization of these costs, or stating the same thing in opposite terms, the maximization of the benefit. Clearly, neither method is perfect, and clearly, we are choosing between two techniques that will produce less than if we

THEORY

lived in a perfect world. There is no reason to be terribly upset about this; most institutions and devices we use lack theoretical perfection.

Finally, it should be noted that although improvements in market organization are rather hard to find today, there are a great many improvements possible in governmental activities. Even though we may now regard the costs of governmental activities as being excessive with respect to some activity, it is possible that with improved governmental design we could reduce the governmental cost and hence make it desirable to shift this activity from the private to the public sector. Still, as things exist today, it would appear that there are a great many activities presently being carried on by governmental agencies that could reasonably be shifted to the market sphere.

# 6

# Remedies

This chapter examines the various remedies that can be applied when externalities exist; the following chapters then consider specific problems in which we can apply our newly acquired knowledge. It must be remembered, of course, that selecting a suitable institution to deal with an externality, in a sense is playing God. In the real world, these decisions are likely to be made either by governments or by businessmen. Neither is free from error; mistakes are made. Furthermore, the decision-making processes used in democratic governments insure a suboptimal outcome. Nevertheless, we should consider what can be done on the assumption that we can make a perfect choice of institutions. Later we can examine the institutions of the real world and make recommendations that are not totally unrealistic.

Let me begin by describing three institutional arrangements that I think are not normally considered by economists. The first of these is exemplified by Belvedere Park where I spent most of my summers as a boy. About fifty years before I was born, some people (living mainly in the town of Belvedere, Illinois) had purchased a plot of land on Lake Geneva in southern Wisconsin. The plot was about 500 feet wide and almost a mile long with the 500-foot frontage on the lake and the other end on what, at that time, was the only available access road. It was a very attractive piece of real estate. Lake Geneva is a beautiful lake, and the tract was not only wooded throughout, but a small stream began about 1,000 feet from the lake and wound (receiving numerous small tributaries) down to the lake entirely within the strip.

The owners of the land formed a corporation. Each building lot carried with it a share of the corporation. These lots were placed in two lines along the side of the strip from very close to the lake shore to about the head-waters of the small stream. Thus, the owner of each of these lots (about forty) not only had the right to build a house on his particular lot, but also had considerable influence on the environment in which that building would stand.[1] By the time that I became old enough to notice Belvedere Park at all, this institution had been in existence for a fairly long period of time and had developed into what one might call a climax form. Naturally, I did not realize that there was anything particularly remarkable about this organization, and unfortunately as a child I did not observe it carefully enough so that I can be absolutely certain that everything I relate here is true. Nevertheless, I think that this is an accurate account.

As I have said, the houses were arranged along the edge of the tracts in two long lines at right angles to the shore of the lake. The lots nearest to the lake were the most valuable and had been sold at correspondingly higher orig-

---

[1] There were some restrictions on the type of building that could be constructed.

inal sale prices. In general, the quality of the houses tended to decline as one went farther away from the lake. Nevertheless, each householder held a share of the stock, and by the time I arrived on the scene there had been some concentration of ownership. Several people owned more than one house and therefore had several votes. Thus, as in most corporations, there was weighted voting. In general, the houses were located on very small plots, not because they were particularly crowded, but because a center strip about 350 feet wide was maintained as a park. This center strip, which contained practically all of the main stream, although not of its tributaries, was gardened by the park. The park mowed the lawns of the house lots, although gardening around the houses was done by the individual householder. My grandmother, who owned the cottage in which I used to spend my summers, was very proud of the rare ferns that she had coaxed into growing directly under the front porch of her cottage. She also was able to raise watercress in a small tributary stream that was one of the boundaries of her lot.

Since the park had first been formed, another road had been built much closer to the lake than the original road so that the park now consisted of two tracts on either side of the new road. All of the cottages were located between the lake and the road. On the other side of the road there were some tennis courts, a number of garages, an open-air parking lot, and a rather large club building that had once been used for social purposes and was still intermittently used for this purpose at the time I was there. Basically, however, during my childhood, the clubhouse was a place where boats were stored and where the children could play on rainy days. It performed both of these functions admirably. The long strip of woodland leading up to the other road was also, of course, a place where the children could amuse themselves.

Basically, however, most of the children's play and indeed most of the social activities of the camp in general revolved around the lakefront where the camp maintained two small piers for rowboats and one large pier for swimming. A resident of the camp had built a rather elaborate diving float, and this was anchored off the pier. Another resident had, with the permission of the camp council, built a small private pier to accommodate his speed boat. This small private pier was also available to anyone who wanted to use it for swimming or fishing. All of these piers had to be dismantled in the fall, stored, and then rebuilt in the spring. This was, of course, done by the camp.

The waterfront as a whole was owned collectively by the camp. It was the custom around Lake Geneva for all pieces of property on the waterfront to maintain footpaths about ten or fifteen feet from the shore. This meant that it was possible for energetic members to walk completely around the lake, a distance of about twenty miles. Some public utilities were provided in the camp, but in a rather unusual way. An access road from the main road had been built by the park and was kept in good condition. There were continual problems about the parking rules with respect to this access road. As a general rule, the continual small changes in the parking regulations were motivated by the fact that the road was really too narrow for permanent parking but that almost everyone found it convenient to park their car in front of their house to load and unload. Attempts at developing a set of rules that would permit people to load and unload from their cars but would not result in so many cars being stopped on the road that traffic was impossible led, as I suppose was predictable, to a long series of petty bickerings and petty changes in the rules.

Electricity was provided by a local private utility. Individual householders purchased their electricity directly but the corporation was responsible for ensuring that the utility did not place its poles down the central park. The electricity was delivered by poles running along the property line behind the houses, and hence did not affect the pleasant appearance of the camp. Water was, oddly enough, an individual matter left to each householder. When I was a small boy, rams in the main stream were the principal source of water with each house having its own ram. Gradually, as I grew older, these rams were replaced by electric pumps. I can recall to this day the chorus of a dozen rams in the stream in front of my grandmother's house. Their replacement by electric pumps was, no doubt, efficient but a very distinct reduction of a positive externality.

Sewage was, in general, also privately provided, with the cottages each having a private septic tank. The corporation was, of course, very much interested in the possibility of contamination of householder A's spring by waste from householder B's septic tank, and engaged in fairly close supervision of the location and design of the septic tanks. There was, oddly enough, another small collective enterprise in the camp. About eight of the cottages that were near the lake had built a very large joint septic tank. This small additional corporation was apparently handled quietly on a cooperative basis by the houses that had provided it. My grandmother's house was not one of them, and therefore I know very little about this institution.

The camp itself provided substantially all local governmental services. Since it was occupied only during the summer when students would normally be on vacation, schooling was not provided. What little police protection was needed was obtained by arranging for one of the men in the camp to be a deputy sheriff equipped with a badge and a gun. So far as I know, neither of these two items was ever used. Substantially, there was no fire protection except insofar as the local water supplies were quite sizable. Furthermore, the camp provided certain other "public services." For example, on the Fourth of July the camp purchased and set off an elaborate display of fireworks. Various other social activities were organized by the entire camp or by small groups of people within the camp. The formal government of the immediate area appeared only as an exploiter. A small village located about a mile from the camp had arranged to hold all of its elections in the winter when the camp would be empty. It then annexed a sizable portion of the shoreline of Lake Geneva, including Belvedere Park, and taxed this area for its own benefit. We, of course, received the general benefits of the state and national government.

The intriguing feature of this institution, from the standpoint of present-day economics, is the very neat way in which it internalized a very large number of externalities that we normally either think of as problems that cannot be solved or as political issues. Furthermore, it is of considerable interest that the particular services that were collectively provided by this "voluntary government" were in many ways quite different from those that are traditional. Perhaps as a holdover from my boyhood experience in this area, I tend to think that if there were very small governmental units (of which more is said in the latter part of this chapter) collective gardening might become much more common than it is today. The problem of the rosebushes that we have now discussed several times could be relatively easily dealt with if all the people in a given small neighborhood were organized in some kind of collective entity.

But let me turn to my second institutional arrangement. Once again, and this will also be true of my third, it is an institution with which I have had considerable personal contact. It is, in fact, the apartment house in which I formerly lived (2016 Main, Houston, Texas). This large apartment house also had as one of its major objectives the internalization of a large collection of externalities. In the first place, the owners had designed the apartment house in such a way that the walls, if not completely soundproof, were sufficiently close to that objective so that we did not annoy our neighbors even if we made quite a bit of noise in our apartments. Secondly, they had provided us with an elaborate set of communal facilities for our use. There was an extremely handsome entry foyer, for example, which was not only attractive but was used also for various social events. Social life, in general, was actively organized by the management of the apartment house. Free coffee and rolls were provided on Sunday morning to all tenants, and a hostess was provided who made strong efforts to promote "socialization" among the tenants. Furthermore, the management had made arrangements so that there would be a coffee shop, a small store that sold food and incidentals, and even a barber shop and a nightclub on the premises. I am sure all of these things operated at a loss, but the management apparently believed that providing these special services to their tenants increased the value of the property as a whole.

Needless to say, the management at 2016 Main also provided a large number of other services. Indoor parking space, maid service if you wanted it, and laundry facilities both through an office of a local laundry and dry cleaning establishment and coin-operated washing and drying equipment on the premises. There was a ceramics course available for those who wished to take it, and a recreation room in which people could hold parties. The management also made arrangements for regular bridge sessions in order to promote social relations among its tenants, and an art show was recently held.

Altogether, 2016 Main is another example of the internalization of externalities. It is, in fact, a rather small example. The same kind of thing on a much larger scale is now becoming common in the United States, in which designed communities owned by one landlord and having a population of 30,000 people are not unknown. Generally speaking, such communities find that the necessity of paying taxes for a number of governmental services, whether or not they themselves provide these services, makes it impossible for them to provide a full line of such services. Nevertheless, they do internalize a number of externalities that are not internalized in the ordinary community and probably could do an excellent job of providing many of these governmental services.

To anticipate some discussion mentioned later in the book, one of the objectives of the urban renewal program in the United States is the creation of the possibility for this type of internalization of externalities. Land that is now divided into a number of small plots is condemned by the government and then resold as a unit to someone who will develop it as a whole. The program has not worked very well, but this seems to be a case of bad management, and not an inherent characteristic.[2]

[2] The program at the moment is in disrepute in the United States, because it does seem to have been used to a very large extent for the purpose of removing Negro communities from places where they are inconvenient from the standpoint of the whites. The title "Negro Removal" has been given to the program by a great many people of liberal bent.

My third institutional system is one I observed while I was in China, but in fact in variant forms it is characteristic of the whole of Asia from, roughly speaking, Persia to the northern boundary of Manchuria.[3] In China the bulk of the population are farmers who live in the country. Traditionally they were organized in small, basically self-governing, villages, which combined with a centralized despotism—for the higher level of government has apparently arisen from what Karl Wittfogel refers to as "declining marginal returns on administration."[4] These local communities were, of course, creatures of the despotic central government and had to be responsive to its wishes, but central government was relatively weak in China. Central government was not greatly concerned about such matters as the placement of a road in a village, the location of a school, or the amount of tax to be raised for *local* facilities. Consequently, these small, self-governing local governments in fact have had a very high degree of autonomy.

The interesting feature of this institution is that these small village organizations (which do not really seem to be much different from the organizations existing in New England) were retained for large cities. A large city in China is legally simply a unit of the same sort as a similar population unit would have in the countryside. There are varying numbers of small neighborhoods that have similar powers and the same type of self-government as they would have if they were villages in the countryside. Such neighborhoods are then grouped into circuits and counties in the same way they would be if they were in the country-

[3] Perhaps I should say *was* characteristic. It may be in process of complete destruction today. In my opinion this will be a most unfortunate example of *The Cost of Economic Growth*, Edward J. Mishan (New York: Frederick A. Praeger, Inc., 1967).

[4] Karl Wittfogel, *Oriental Despotism* (New Haven: Yale University Press, 1954).

side. Under the old imperial government, for example, the city of Peking was legally about 3,000 villages grouped into 3 counties. Thus, the Chinese attitude is that local matters should be dealt with locally; and by locally they mean by some small group of people, not by the city of Peking acting as a whole. They would not quarrel with the statement that there are a number of matters that cannot be dealt with at this level, but they realize that there are a number that can be.

Once again, this general institution spreads over much of Asia and is also found in India and Indonesia. In the cities there are little clusters, which, perhaps without any legal recognition at all, are to a considerable extent self-governing. Needless to say, their powers are never so impressive as to significantly reduce the control of the central government, but they do provide a method of dealing with many local problems at the local level. It seems to me that this is an institution that we could well copy in the Western world. If areas of a few blocks were permitted to establish their own little governmental agency to take care of such matters as street cleaning, and perhaps the purchase of public utilities in the wholesale market, as well as doing some supplementary gardening, and controlling the entire range of things that Mishan refers to as "amenities," it seems to me that many externalities could be eliminated.

Such local governments have a further advantage such as that found in some communities in the United States even though we do not have these very small "village" organizations in our cities. That advantage is the possibility of moving if one dislikes the government of a particular community. Thus, it is possible to develop decentralized communities catering to different tastes. In general, the smaller such communities are, the better they would be able to cater to specialized tastes but the fewer externalities they would be able to internalize. On the other hand, in a massive city such as New York, it would seem reasonable that not only would there be organizations dealing with the problems of a few blocks, but also larger subdivisions dealing with larger problems.

As far as I can see from the examination of public opinion polls, Harlem, for example, would be much better governed if the inhabitants had control over a great range of the public services they now receive. It seems certain that they would acquire an all-Black police force, but it seems equally certain that this all-Black police force would then proceed to establish law and order in areas where the present police force does not. Furthermore, the issue of police brutality would not arise. The people who are now most injured by the state of public order in Harlem are the inhabitants of Harlem, and the public opinion data indicate that they are fully aware of this.

It is probably the racial overtones of the problem that have led a great many people in the United States to turn toward the development of neighborhood governments within the present cities. It would, indeed, benefit the Negro communities in such places as New York and Chicago, but we should not assume that that is its principal advantage. It also seems likely that, in general, these Negro communities themselves are large enough so that a great many services should be controlled at a smaller, or "block" level. Obviously, communities that are all white or that have some other ethnic coloration would also be better governed if there were neighborhood control of a number of problems. It should be emphasized again that these very small local governments would not only be able to carry on some of the present-day activities in a way that is more in accord with local preferences, but it seems likely that they would also be able to undertake various additional activities.

The cities of New York and Houston, for example, must, to a considerable extent, provide the same service throughout the city, which means that for many activities it would be wiser for an individual to keep complete control himself rather than to transfer control to such a large organization. If he were given the alternative of transferring control to a small organization, close to his own interest and in which his own vote is actually a significant matter, he might well find that further services should be transferred to collective control. I have mentioned gardening and mowing lawns, and it does seem to me that these are particularly obvious examples.

Note that the use of small governmental units would not make it particularly difficult to obtain the advantages of normal economies of scale. There is no reason why these small governmental units should not enter into contracts with larger agencies to provide specialized service as is now done, for example, by many small cities in Los Angeles County. The problem here, of course, is one of what we have called contiguity rather than the economies of scale. When there are only economies of scale, when a large producer can produce more cheaply than a small producer, there is no reason why a very small local community should not purchase from the large producer. When, however, efficient production requires that the large areas all receive exactly the same service from exactly the same producer, then we have the contiguity problem, a special type of externality, and it is no longer possible to obtain economies by contract. It may still be possible, however, for a group of small governmental units to organize a cooperative to provide the services. Nevertheless, as the number of small units increases, the bargaining problems also increase, and it becomes more difficult to attain voluntary agreement. It must be noted, however, that our experience with the suburbs would seem to indicate that the very elaborate and complex governmental arrangements providing specialized services can be negotiated among large numbers of small governmental units.

The existence of many small governmental units provides an opportunity for a wide diversity of services and hence for a good deal more satisfaction for the citizens who are permitted to choose from among these services, but it is unlikely that this wide diversity will be fully utilized as long as the individual units are democratic. As stated previously, there are a number of reasons why voters are unlikely to bother to thoroughly inform themselves. Furthermore, the voters have only relatively weak motives for attempting to attract other people into their district or to prevent people from leaving it. Thus, they are unlikely to attempt to produce a specialized set of municipal services in order to attract people into the area. A private corporation that somehow had control of the government might be motivated to produce a combination of services that was considerably different from the standard set in order to appeal to a minority. Thus, the provision of a wide diversity of services by local governments probably is not possible under present institutions. It would seem desirable to experiment by permitting individual companies to provide the full range of government services in small areas in order to make possible this greater diversity. As long as the areas were small and anyone could move out of them, there does not seem to be any obvious reason why such experiments would endanger anyone's rights.

THEORY

Another problem raised by the use of small governmental units, or indeed, by any method of eliminating externalities that does not take in the entire solar system, is the boundary between units. Insofar as two adjacent governmental units are dealing with the same externality in much the same way, it may well be that the boundary between the two communities will have no observable effects. If, however, the two communities decide to deal with a problem differently (one, for example, by deciding it doesn't want to worry about mosquitoes and the other by having a highly active mosquito abatement program), then there will be externalities at the border of the units. The cost of these externalities certainly should be considered and weighed against the advantages of obtaining a degree of mosquito abatement that is in close accord with the desires of the people who are in each of the governmental units. One does not wish to internalize all externalities. A finite possibility exists that some person from Afghanistan will meet you and be offended by your clothing. This externality could only be dealt with by giving the Afghans some control over your choice of shirts. Most people would agree that in this case the externality is of less importance than the preferences of the "local unit."

This discussion has been merely a cursory examination of three institutional arrangements that should be given greater consideration. Let us now turn to an examination of the technical methods of reducing externalities. In general, if I feel that someone is causing me external costs or that by altering his behavior he could provide me with greater external economies than I now receive, I have two methods of influencing his action. The first of these is to attempt to arrange some kind of agreement with him on a private basis, the second is to attempt to manipulate the

142

government into action. My choice between these two methods will normally involve a judgment on my part as to their cost and benefit. A second question that I must consider is exactly what kind of change I want in order to alter his behavior. I might, for example, want to have him completely desist from doing something or I might simply be interested in his paying me compensation for doing it. There are, as we shall see later, many different ways in which such problems can be dealt with.

Let us, however, begin by considering the private or governmental choice. Traditionally, I think, governmental action was distinguished from private action on the grounds that governmental action is backed by force and private action characteristically is not. Recently, some scholars have been distinguishing between collective action and private action in terms of the decision process. Private action, in this view, requires unanimous assent; collective action is based upon a decision process other than that requiring unanimous agreement. Either of these definitions raises problems. I can, for example, hire a private police force that will make use of force to protect my property as many people have done. In using the force definition, it is difficult to decide whether this is a government or private act.

I prefer the distinction based on the presence or absence of a requirement of unanimous assent; but with this definition, a great many things that are normally referred to as private, that is, corporations, are called collective. For the remainder of the chapter, however, let us ignore these difficult problems and follow common practice.

Turning then to the actual procedures that may be used, the simplest way of dealing with an externality is to make some change in the property arrangements. Suppose that my neighbor is proposing to construct a building that will cut off my view. I can approach him and offer to pay him a sum of money to give me the air rights over his plot; that is, to sell me that part of his "landholding" that is more than thirty feet above the surface. He can then no longer build a building at that level without my permission. The property that he holds has been transferred in part to me. Approximately the same situation can be handled in another way. I could pay my neighbor to add a covenant to his deed not to erect a building more than thirty feet high and provide that this covenant will remain in the deed in future sales of the property to other persons.

This type of covenant, restricting the use of property, is common, and frequently complex and detailed. Residential property in particular is likely to be subject to such covenants for the purpose of usually preventing the generation of negative externalities on neighboring property. This widespread activity is the most common single method of reducing the number of short-range externalities. As far as I know, it has not been thoroughly studied by economists, but it surely would repay a good deal of serious research.

As we have noted a number of times before, bargaining is extremely difficult if a number of persons are involved. Thus, if an externality is evident that affects a number of people and/or is generated by a number of people, it is unlikely that we will be able to enter into such a private bargain. In this case, I might rationally attempt to lobby the government into doing something about the matter. The government remedy might, however, also be a modification of property rights. One of the normal activities of government is to define and enforce property rights, although it can, of course, change these property definitions.

An obvious example of this modification would be the

development of setback rules in our larger cities. The early builders of skyscrapers held rather literally to the view that they owned all the space over their land and simply built skyscrapers that covered the entire surface of the ground. Anyone who has visited Wall Street in New York City is aware of the rather gloomy effect of this type of architecture.

Eventually the city government, in essence, confiscated part of the airspace above any plot of land in New York. Setback rules were enacted that made it impossible for the owner of property in New York to build an extremely tall building on all of his property. He must taper his building inwardly at the upper floors in order to avoid cutting off light and air from his neighbors. These laws clearly altered what the individual owned. They redefined property in an effort to reduce the generation of negative externalities by a person on his neighbor's property. Since the externality was reciprocal, it is quite probable that the restriction actually increased the value of the real estate involved.

Zoning restrictions are, of course, another obvious example, but consider also the building lines in most cities. In most residential areas, each street has a specified building line past which owners are prohibited from building houses farther forward on their lots. The object of the prohibition, of course, is to provide sizeable front lawns and thus generate a pleasant effect. It is a clear example of regulating "gardening" in order to produce a positive externality. The prospects for reducing externalities by changing property laws are apparently almost infinite. The unitization of oil pools is one example, but there are many others. Our present property laws have largely developed through historical accretion, and there is no strong reason to believe that they are anywhere near optimal. Changes in the law may well be desirable.

There are, however, two disadvantages to any proposal for government changes of property laws. The first of these, of course, is that the mere discussion of such changes generates externalities. If I purchase a piece of property and do not know whether or not the government may make radical changes in the bundle of rights that I have purchased, I incur a substantial risk from that uncertainty. Minimizing this risk would appear to be something that would be a desirable reduction of externalities. In general, this can be done if any change in property rights requires condemnation proceedings with payment of full compensation. Any change in the law of property that reduces externalities will confer more benefits than its cost, and hence there is always a theoretical possibility of fully compensating everyone injured and at the same time making a profit. Compensation, then, should normally be required.[5]

The second problem is that if we turn to the government as an instrument for changing people's property rules, then the voters may make use of the government instrumentality not only to change property rules but also to transfer resources to themselves. For example, the setback laws in New York City were simply enacted. No compensation was paid to the owners who found that their rights had been to some extent restricted, nor was a tax placed on the beneficiaries. It was a transfer of assets among the owners

[5] Another technique, suggested by Mishan, is simply to provide that the law take effect, say, seven years in the future. The present value of the change would be slight, and everyone would have seven years in which to adjust.

of real estate. It should, then, be kept in mind that a governmental agency that has been called into some area in order to reduce externalities may, in fact, do more. It may well be more interested in transferring income to powerfully situated political groups and perhaps actually create further externalities if there is some political advantage to be gained.

As has already been pointed out, there is no reason to believe that the government will choose an optimal policy with respect to the externality. Presumably the decision processes will produce an outcome which may very well be better than that obtained in the market. It may, however, be worse. As was pointed out in the first chapter, if the members of the community have relatively similar tastes and the externality is a large one, it is likely that government action will improve matters. If tastes are widely varying and the externality is a small one, it is likely that governmental action will be worse than market provision. In any given case, we could theoretically make precise calculations, predict the outcome under governmental and private provision, and then decide which of the two institutional sets was better. It is unfortunate, but true, that such calculations have almost never been undertaken.

A second method that can be used to deal with an externality is a rule regulating the action of some person or persons. It may be noted that there is a gray area between the first method, the change of property definition, and the second method of rules. A provision that I may not do something on my property could well be described either as a rule restricting my action or as changing the nature of my title to the property. The reason for mentioning the rule process is not because I want to make any subtle distinction here, but because there are a number of rules that reduce externalities and that do not seem to be very closely connected to any property institution.

Many American cities, for example, require that dog owners inoculate their dogs against rabies. It is difficult, although not impossible, to describe this as a modification of the property laws. Requiring individuals to undertake actions that will produce positive externalities for others or reduce negative externalities is common in the world at large. In many parts of the world, the streets are kept clean by requiring the householders to clean that part of the street in front of their house. Many laws also prohibit people from engaging in conduct that would be offensive to the rest of the community. There are minimum standards in the amount of clothing worn in public, and even, to some extent, on the stage. Loud noises at certain times are prohibited, and individuals are under a positive duty to take care to avoid inflicting injury on others.

It is my general impression that this particular way of reducing externalities is less likely to be significant in highly prosperous communities than it is in poorer communities. Still, this is merely my impression and one should not assume without further evidence that as we become more prosperous, this particular method of reducing externalities will be used less frequently. There are, in fact, many economists who feel that this is a growing, rather than a shrinking, field of action.

All of the examples mentioned thus far of the control of individual action in order to reduce externalities have involved the government. As a matter of fact, governmental controls are the largest example of this category, unless we wish to include contracts of employment as examples. Assuming that we do not wish to include such contracts, then this particular method of reducing externalities is relatively rare in the private sector. One can, however, cite some examples. Frequently, when an individual sells a business to someone else, he also agrees that he will not start a new, competing business for a specified term of years. This is clearly an effort to reduce an externality. Easements may contain requirements that the person holding the property subject to the easement take positive action with respect to it. For example, my sister and her husband have recently purchased a plot of land, the only access to which is across the land of another individual. They have been granted an easement across this other land in return for their agreeing to build and maintain a road that will be used both by themselves and the other owner.

Nevertheless, again excepting contracts of employment, I do not think there are very many cases in which the externalities are eliminated by private agreements that simply require a person to do something. Thus, this particular method of reducing externalities is mainly characteristic of governments. In this it is unique. All of the other methods we will discuss are as commonly found in private agreements as they are in government action. It is also unique in that it probably is more subject to abuse for political reasons than any other method of reducing externalities. The cost to the government of compelling an individual to do something or preventing him from doing something is normally very low. Furthermore, the activities to which the government objects are frequently only under certain circumstances externality generating. Suppose, for example, I enjoy drinking myself into a drunken stupor. As long as I do this quietly at home, it disturbs no one. If, however, I choose to drive to the store for another bottle of whiskey (let us say, my fourth for the evening) I am generating a decided externality. In this particular case, our laws recognize the problem and there is substantially no legal restriction on private drunkenness. The laws prohibit drunken driving and public drunkenness. With respect to some drugs, however, this is not so; marijuana and heroin, for example, are illegal even when they do not affect behavior outside the home.

The various restrictions on sexual irregularities are further examples of this method. An individual may well be deeply offended by the knowledge that there is a brothel next door to him. In this sense, the brothel is generating a negative externality for him. If, however, none of the people who are offended by the existence of the brothel discovers that it exists, it generates no negative externality. Nevertheless, our laws do not prohibit brothels whose existence is known to puritans, they prohibit all brothels. Thus, this effort to reduce an externality has been improperly drafted, presumably because the operators of the brothels find themselves in politically difficult positions.

Thus far we have been concerned with the provision of definite rules for controlling conduct. It is also possible to reduce externalities by establishing administrative controls. Instead of Mr. A's activities being controlled by a definite rule, whether contractual or legal, he may be placed under a duty to carry out regulations or administrative orders from an individual or organization in order to reduce the same externality. The fact that almost a quarter of all American retail trade today is organized in this way is a fairly clear example of an externality-reducing activity. Let us, for example, consider the Howard Johnson's "chain." Individual Howard Johnson restaurants are mostly owned by private entrepreneurs who usually live in the same area as the restaurant. The restaurants are, however, all of the same architectural pattern and offer substantially identical menus. This requires that the individual restaurant be subject to careful supervision from the central Howard Johnson organization, and, in fact, the individual restaurant owner pays a substantial fee for this supervision.

Clearly the owner of an individual Howard Johnson restaurant does not benefit greatly from this supervision of his own restaurant. He does receive technical advice that probably improves his efficiency but he would probably be better off if he could slightly reduce the standards of his restaurant and thus obtain a favorable externality from the advertising effect of the other Howard Johnson restaurants operating at a slightly higher quality level. The reason for the detailed regulation is simply to make this reduction of quality impossible. The bulk of Howard Johnson's customers are people driving from one place to another who are not familiar with the local restaurants. They do know, however, almost exactly what they will find at a Howard Johnson. Thus, the behavior of one Howard Johnson restaurant administered by detailed regulation will affect the others, and the internalization of this externality and the provision to the traveler of a highly standardized fare are a valuable service to the customer.

Similar detailed regulation by governmental agencies is not infrequent. For various reasons, at least in the United States, this has not worked out very well. The governmental agencies seem, after a while, to either become hopelessly stodgy and old-fashioned or to develop into organizations that, in essence, operate a cartel for the industry they are allegedly regulating. Sometimes both of these results occur, but the fact that our experience indicates that the government does not do well in this role does not mean that it cannot do so. Neither does it mean that we should

151

not try to improve the efficiency of the governmental agencies conducting it.

But let us proceed to analyze further methods of reducing externalities. The method that I should like to discuss next consists of setting up an organization to provide a service. Here, again, we find that examples of private organizations of this sort are nearly as common as governmental organizations. Earlier I discussed the organization of Belvedere Park, and a great many large apartment buildings or large real estate developments of any sort involve an organization providing special services to its members. When I was a boy I worked as a caddymaster at a golf course, which was owned jointly by the people who had purchased lots in a subdivision lying around the course. It generated significant externalities for its owners. Farmington Country Club, just outside Charlottesville, Virginia, is a spectacular example of this particular way of generating externalities through a golf course. In this case the collectivity is the corporation that originally sold the Farmington lots to the present owners. With great commercial acumen they have been able to time the sale of lots and the changes and additions to the golf course so that they continuously bring new pieces of property into the market in extremely attractive environments. It has been profitable for the owners, and the people who have purchased the property in the country club area also seem to be satisfied with their bargain.

On a smaller scale, arrangements of this sort are frequently found among business organizations. Two or three corporations who need a specialized service will form a special corporation for that purpose. Dow-Corning, for example, was set up by a chemical company and a glass company to deal with a special line of products that involved technologies lying between the lines of the two companies. Dow-Corning has expanded and is now one of the hundred largest corporations in the United States. This was an effort to internalize certain externalities in the research and production capacities of the two corporations. On a smaller scale, trade associations are examples of private persons joining together to set up a special organization that can obtain certain external benefits for them.

In this area, also are found a large portion of the activities of existing governments. The police force is a good example. The government organizes something that proceeds to generate favorable externalities or to eliminate negative externalities (depending upon how you wish to state it) for a great many people. The highway system, national defense, and the weather bureau are other examples. Indeed one can make a list involving a very large part of the activities of both local and national governments as coming under this heading. Here again we have the usual set of problems as to whether or not in a given case a government would provide a better "product" than the private market, and, again, this is a matter of careful calculation.

One special problem should also be briefly discussed. If several people observe an externality and feel that an organization should be established to deal with it, they can either set up the organization themselves or they can contract with someone else to provide the necessary service. Furthermore, they are not confronted with the choice of contracting out the entire organization or setting up an entire organization themselves. They may contract out various parts of it. For example, most roads in the United States are produced by private companies. However, a great deal of the road maintenance is done directly by the government.

Similarly, if we consider private agreements in which an externality is internalized through an organization, we sometimes observe that this is done by contracting it out. The building in which I formerly lived (2016 Main), for example, obtains a number of economies of scale in mechanical maintenance by hiring other specialized corporations to carry out maintenance activities. These specialized corporations obtain their economies of scale by having a large number of similar customers. The choice for 2016 Main between joining together with a large number of other apartment buildings and setting up a special organization that hires plumbers or entering into contract with a company that provides plumbing for them as a unit is clearly the traditional management problem of whether a company should make or buy a component. The same holds true for the government.

As anyone who has read the managerial literature will realize, this is frequently (although not always) an extremely difficult problem and once again little can be said about it in a general way. Careful individual calculations should be made, and it should be emphasized, however, that tradition is not a good guide. Many activities were initially undertaken by the government on its own, rather than by contract. It does not follow that this procedure is efficient. For example, the different branches of the armed services have completely different policies relative to the procurement of weapons: the Army tries to produce everything itself, the Air Force tries to contract out everything, and the Navy has an intermediate position on these matters. There is no evidence that this difference represents any difference in technology; it appears simply to be a result of tradition. What we need is careful calculations and decisions in terms of efficiency in which we should be very careful not to be misled by the dead hand of the past.

The final method of dealing with externalities is one that is relatively little used but that, in recent years, has attracted attention because it appears to be the most efficient way of dealing with a large range of externalities. This method involves changing the prices that the individual enterprise faces by a system of taxes and/or subsidies. We have already discussed this method in connection with a number of individual cases, but it is worthwhile repeating it again. Suppose, for example, that there are a number of companies engaged in dumping polluted waste into a river. Instead of establishing a set of standards for the amount of such waste these companies can put into the river, we tax them. It becomes expensive for them to pollute the river, and they reduce the pollution. Furthermore, this solution permits each individual company to adjust the amount of its pollution to its cost structure. By an appropriate choice of the tax, we can obtain whatever amount of total pollution we wish for the river, while not interfering with the individual company management. This appears to be the most efficient method of pollution control.

Similarly, in an activity that generates positive externalities, we can cause individuals to increase their production by giving them subsidies. To return again to the subject of individual gardens, which surely do create positive externalities for neighbors, a program under which people were subsidized to the extent of (shall we say) one-third of the cost of any flowering bush that they plant in their garden, would lead to an increase in the number of flowering bushes and hence to the "internalization" of the externality. Generally speaking, economists have thought that this method is the most efficient way of dealing with a wide range of externalities, but as I stated previously there do not seem to be a vast number of examples of this method in the real world. The wonderfully conceived organization for controlling the Ruhr River basin is perhaps the best illustration.[6]

An excellent example of this type of subsidy in the private sector is advertising by those enterprises in which the retail unit is a separate business from the manufacturer. If a local Plymouth agency decides to lease a billboard to advertise its wares, it will not only increase its own business but it is likely to some extent to increase the business of all other Plymouth dealers as well. Thus, the externality can be dealt with by subsidization. By any one of a very large number of techniques, the central manufacturer will subsidize local advertising. This is a simple way of internalizing an externality.

In this method, we also have problems in deciding what a governmental agency is likely to do. The subsidy or tax on the externality-generating activity will, unless it is greatly excessive, normally improve the situation over what it was prior to the imposition of the subsidy or tax, but it is difficult to understand why a government would choose the optimal tax or subsidy. My efforts to determine what would happen in a voting context, in which the individuals are both the payers of the subsidy through a tax and the recipients of a subsidy in the sense that a positive externality-generating commodity that they normally purchase will be subsidized, have led to a complicated individual decision process. There does not seem to be anything about this decision process that would lead to the conclusion that the

[6] Allen Kneese, *Water Pollution: Economic Aspects and Research Needs* (Baltimore: Johns Hopkins University Press, 1962).

majority voting outcome would be close to the optimum. Other decision-making procedures seem to be equally unlikely to achieve the optimal adjustment. Since there is a real danger of overtaxation or oversubsidization, it would seem desirable to carry this particular research much further and to obtain fairly definite ideas as to whether or not the governmental decision process may be likely to lead to a situation that is worse than no subsidization at all. Note, however, that it would appear that these investigations are merely a precaution. One would assume that in most cases a modest subsidy or a modest tax would benefit matters. The fact that it would not reach the optimum is unfortunate, but we live in an imperfect world.

This chapter has been devoted to a discussion of the methods of reducing externalities. In the first part, we discussed some organizational methods that are not normally, I think, carefully considered by economists who investigate this problem, and in the second part, we listed the technical possibilities. Clearly, we have a wide range of available methods, and clearly the one that should be applied in any given case is not necessarily an easy decision. We do, however, have a fair margin for error in those cases in which we are dealing with a large externality. If the externality is sizeable, then although we would like to choose the best possible way of dealing with it, we can still benefit from dealing with it by a rather ineptly chosen tool. In general, the larger the externality, the less care we need in choosing the tool. Although we can obtain a benefit from even somewhat inept externality reduction, we will obtain a greater benefit if we are able to more efficiently design the externality-reducing activity.

# PART

# II

# PRACTICE

# Merely Pecuniary

Thus far this book has been mainly devoted to a general discussion of the modern theory of government. Our basic objective has been a theoretical development of the tools that could be used in order to make the basic decision between governmental and private provision. We have occasionally applied these tools to concrete problems, but in those cases in which we have applied these tools, our objective has been merely to clarify the theory. Part II applies the principles developed in Part I to the real world. In this chapter we will deal with a number of areas in which phenomena occur that appear to be externalities, but where economists are agreed that governmental action to reduce the externality is undesirable. Indeed most economists would argue that even private persons should be prohibited by law from attempting to reduce these externalities.

The traditional explanation of why we do not attempt to reduce externalities in this area has been to say that they are "merely pecuniary." This phrase has never impressed me as being self-explanatory and therefore I wish to develop the reasons in a somewhat more careful way. The professional expert in this field may regard this chapter as unduly tedious, but it should be helpful to people who have not devoted a great deal of time and energy to this particular field of learning.[1]

Suppose I am a merchant and that I decide to lower the prices on an article that I am selling. My new low prices will attract a number of customers. While this involves transactions between me and my customers, it also injures a third party, in fact a number of third parties. My competitors lose part of their business, and hence by applying our literal definition of externality, this is an externality. Many governments have thought that this particular type of externality required governmental action. In much of the world, potential new businesses must obtain the permission of the existing businesses, and government controls of prices are common. These phenomena are seldom found in Anglo-Saxon countries, but are not at all uncommon on the continent of Europe. By preventing a newcomer from entering a particular line of business, the prospect that the people now in the business will be driven into bankruptcy or in some other way injured by aggressive salesmanship on his part is eliminated. Once again, what would appear to be an externality is controlled.

In the United States, we seldom find this simple rule under which existing enterprises have the right to prevent the entry of others but we, not uncommonly, have governmental agencies that perform the same function. The Inter-

---

[1] For those who wish to know more on this subject see Roland N. McKean, *Efficiency in Government Through Systems Analysis* (New York: John Wiley & Sons, 1958), pp. 134-147, which contains an excellent discussion.

state Commerce Commission prevents new entrants into the trucking business; the Civil Aeronautics Board prevents new entrants into the air transportation business; and the Department of Agriculture sharply restricts the production of agricultural products. Barbering, medicine, drycleaning, and undertaking are all "beneficiaries" of this kind of governmental control. In all of these cases, it is certainly true that "tough competition" would injure certain people.

Most economists, however, regard this particular type of externality as one we should not attempt to eliminate, and they become rather indignant when they discuss the behavior of the Interstate Commerce Commission, the Civil Aeronautics Board, or the innumerable local boards that restrict entry into all sorts of minor professions. They are also extremely critical of laws such as those in Austria that make it almost impossible to start new enterprises without the permission of the existing businesses. Granted that a potential price cutter will most assuredly not consider the damage that he may inflict on his competitors, but why do economists ignore the externality problem? [2] The simplest explanation is shown in Figure 11. Let us suppose that the existing producers are selling Q units at price P, and the new producer, who undercuts, charges price P.' At this price, Q' units can be sold. This means an injury to the existing producers, which is, roughly speaking, the dotted rectangle. The customers also gain, of course, by the dotted rectangle and the shaded triangle and it is clear that the total gain is greater than the loss.

Mishan is almost unique among economists in arguing that in some cases, especially capital exports, controls that impede new entry in order to keep prices up are desirable.

[2] If he does consider it, he is apt to regard it as a positive advantage.

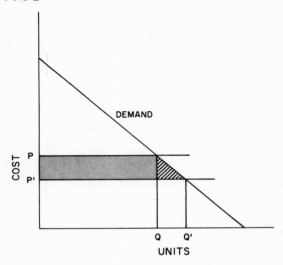

FIGURE 11. The Welfare Triangle

For the world economy as a whole this reduction in the returns of all intramarginal units represents a transfer from the owners of capital to the rest of the population, but from the standpoint of a capital exporting country, the fall in the return of the intramarginal units of capital already exported is to be regarded as an external diseconomy. For the additional investor unwittingly reflects the loss on all existing holders of foreign capital. Such a loss would be taken into account only if the export of capital were in the hands of a monopoly.[3]

Note that Mishan considers the fall in the return in capital an externality only for one group, the capital exporting country. Surely, however, the reduction on the return on capital is a bona fide externality for everyone. For many (particularly foreigners) it is an external economy, not a cost.

[3] Edward J. Mishan, *The Cost of Economic Growth* (New York: Frederick A. Praeger, Inc., 1967), footnote, p. 23.

Why do we not require that the price cutter compensate his competitors? First, it is impossible for the new producer to do so because in order to obtain the dotted rectangle, he would have to charge as high a price as the original producers were charging. He could, however, enter into an agreement with the customers to jointly buy out the original producers. However, this situation involves the problem of bargaining costs, and most people would agree that these costs are excessive. One might conclude, however, that it would be proper to have the government purchase the right to cut prices from the existing producers and then collect by taxation the area of the dotted rectangle from the customers. Theoretically, there is no objection to this, but it is not what we observe in actual practice. More exactly it is not what we usually observe. There are occasions when it is done; there are cases in which the government condemns an existing monopoly and compensates the owners.

Normally, however, we do not see this kind of government intervention. Repeating the slogan "merely pecuniary" does not help. There is, however, a perfectly good argument for this policy. The process of condemnation and collection of the cost by the government through taxes would necessarily be an uncertain one. The gain to society (the small triangle) is fairly certain to be relatively small.[4] Thus, there would be a considerable government tax to gain a rather small amount, and it seems probable that the government would frequently miscalculate. In the long run, it can be assumed fairly safely that the average person will confront this situation many times; sometimes as a seller who is undercut and sometimes as a customer who gains

[4] See Harvey Leibenstein, "Allocative Efficiency vs. 'X-Efficiency'," *American Economic Review*, 56 (June 1966): 392–415.

from the undercutting. One would anticipate that during most people's lifetimes there would be a net gain by permitting undercutting.

But if we decide not to compel people who wish to cut prices or open new enterprises that will injure existing enterprises to pay compensation, the question still exists as to whether we should permit enterprises to enter into voluntary agreements to eliminate this externality. Once again, we find that many governments have decided that this is a desirable policy. Until very recently the United States was unique in having government institutions that made this type of agreement dangerous. In the last few years American antitrust policy has been widely copied in various parts of the world. Nevertheless, it is probably still true that such agreements are legal in more countries of the world than in those countries that have active antimonopoly policies.

Here we have individuals attempting to internalize certain externalities, that is, prevent undercutting, and the question is whether this activity should be made illegal. We should begin by noting that there is an externality, no matter how we arrange the institutions. If we permit people to undercut, this means that they enter into an agreement with their customers that injures competitors. If, on the other hand, we permit all the producers of a commodity to enter into an agreement to eliminate undercutting, this injures their customers. Once again, if we turn to Figure 10, we can see what one might call the standard economic argument for being opposed to this type of agreement that eliminates at least one kind of externality. Assume that a competitive market would produce quantity $Q'$ at price $P.'$ The producers enter into an agreement to raise the price to P, which leads to a transfer from the customers to the producers of the dotted rectangle, but also leads to an unambiguous net loss to society equivalent to the shaded triangle. Thus, it can be demonstrated that the total loss arising in a society from this agreement is greater than the gain received by its beneficiaries. Most economists in recent times have used this as an argument for prohibiting this particular type of externality-reducing private agreement.

If the formation of monopolies is permitted, this is an agreement that individuals may, by proper organization, obtain an income equivalent to the dotted rectangle. The capital value of this income would normally be a large sum of money, and one would anticipate that people would invest large resources in efforts to obtain this income. Furthermore, much of this would involve competitive squabbling between different enterprises, each desiring to obtain the monopoly for itself, or at least a larger share of the market. This investment of resources would be a pure social waste. Thus, permitting the activity of "monopolizing" (whether the monopoly is formed through direct private action or through lobbying to arrange government sanctions to support the monopoly) is likely to incur large social costs.[5] So far, we seem to have developed a rationalization for prohibiting the elimination of certain externalities. We must, of course, note that many nations have regarded the reduction of these particular externalities as a suitable activity for government, but American economic tradition does not favor it. Let us, however, consider some further implications of the reasoning we have so far undertaken. Let us suppose that Mr. Smith proposes to begin a

---

[5] See Gordon Tullock, "The Welfare Costs of Monopolies, Tariffs, and Theft," *Western Economics Journal*, 5, no. 3 (June 1967): 224–232.

new enterprise that is more efficient than the existing enterprises in his particular line of business, and hence that he will be able to lower prices to the customer. Let us further suppose that Mr. Smith can prove that the prices can be lowered even further if he can build his building where Mr. Jones now has a house. Under these circumstances, there would be a significant welfare gain from the construction of Mr. Smith's building where Mr. Jones' house now stands. The argument we have posed thus far would seem to indicate that Mr. Smith could, therefore, take over Mr. Jones' house without paying him any compensation. The real estate will move to a "higher use" and there will be a net welfare gain. Why then should we insist that under these circumstances Mr. Smith must pay Mr. Jones for his building?

The first impulse of the reader is probably that I am asking a totally absurd question. We are so accustomed to compensation in such a case that it does not seem to require explanation; it is difficult to comprehend why anyone should even raise the problem. As we shall see, however, there is an area of public policy in which precisely this question does arise and where it is in fact extremely difficult to solve. In our simple private business case, however, it is clear that although there will be bargaining costs (Mr. Smith must compensate Mr. Jones) that would not otherwise exist, nevertheless, it is a two-party bargain, and these costs are not likely to be excessive. If Mr. Smith was given the right to confiscate Mr. Jones' building if he could prove that he could make a more efficient use of the property, he would, in the first place, have a considerable investment in the proceedings before the board that ruled on such matters. There is no obvious reason to believe that the bargaining costs would be more of a burden on society than this proceeding.

A more fundamental objection to transferring the property without compensation, however, is concerned with the externality of the transfer process itself. If I own some piece of property, (and it need not be real estate; it can be personal property) and I feel secure in my possession of that property, I am likely to pay considerable attention to increasing its value in various ways. If, on the other hand, the legal institutions are such that anyone who can demonstrate he has a "superior" usage for the property can take it from me without paying me compensation, then it is likely that I will be less motivated to invest capital and/or resources in improving it. Since human judgment is not perfect, I might miscalculate and put some resources into the property that do not return an optimal output. Someone else, *ex post*, could observe that my output was not optimal and therefore propose to take over the property. Under the circumstances, I would not invest my resources in improving the property but would instead invest them in vacations on the Riviera.

Thus, in those cases in which bargaining costs are relatively modest, that is, where there are small numbers of parties involved, we generally believe that compensation should be paid. In our society we have a number of cases, however, in which bargaining costs would be great. The normal method of dealing with them is through condemnation. Two examples, the urban renewal program and highway building, both proceed through condemnation because it is thought that the bargaining problems would be excessive. A piece of property that is thought to be suitable for a highway can normally not be purchased at a reasonable price by direct bargaining because once a good portion of the highway has been purchased, the holders of the remaining property are in a position to extort extremely high prices by threatening to force the highway into expensive detours.

Similarly, the urban renewal program is based on the belief that a large area of deteriorated property with each piece of property held by a separate owner is unlikely to be the center of improvement. Each individual landholder realizes that improvement to his property would, in part, redound to the benefit of his neighbors and that the poor condition of his neighbor's property injures his. He, therefore, does not invest money in improving the land. By pooling the land over a large area under a single owner, it is possible (or at least so some of the proponents of this program claim) to internalize these externalities and the property can therefore be improved. In both of these cases, we condemn the property and pay compensation.

The question naturally arises as to why we find it necessary to pay compensation and how we decide what compensation to pay. Why not simply take the property as was done by the old Chinese Imperial government? [6] If it is true that there is a social benefit from change in the property ownership, then the argument for breaking up monopolies without compensation would seem to apply here. In any event, the situation could be analyzed once again by Figure 11. If there is no such social gain, then surely the government should not take the property. It seems likely that the reason for having government payment in these areas is partly because of a strong feeling of justice, which is something an economist can hardly deal

---

[6] Nominally all property was held by lease from the crown, so the operation taken legally was simply a termination of a lease.

with, and partly the desire to give reasonable security to the investment of resources in improving land.

In any event, the actual decision as to what compensation shall be paid is an extremely difficult one. "Uncompensated Non-Construction Costs which Urban Highways and Urban Renewal Impose upon Residential Households," by Anthony Downs, is a careful survey of the problem by a man who knows a great deal about the subject, and it is notable that he finds that a large number of values are taken in condemnation proceedings without being compensated.[7] Downs attempts to develop rules for deciding when compensation should and should not be paid. In my opinion, these rules are not very satisfactory, although this is not said in any critical spirit. The rules proposed by Downs are the best that I have seen and certainly far better than any that I could prepare. It nevertheless does seem to me that we have a number of mysteries that would repay a good deal of further research.

Nevertheless, it must be conceded that there are many externalities that we wish to retain. If I were to make a general statement as to the areas in which we find these "merely pecuniary" externalities, I would say it is those areas in which traditional economics offered good solutions. For example, the argument for competition is an old one, and the argument for government condemnation with compensation for certain types of property is equally old. Perhaps as a result of mere tradition, perhaps as a result of the considerations that we have discussed, and perhaps as the result of other reasons that have escaped my search, most economists refuse to apply the concept of externality in the areas that we have been discussing and argue that individual behavior in which individuals ignore some of

[7] Privately circulated manuscript.

171

PRACTICE

the effects their behavior has on others is more desirable than compelling them to take these effects into account. I do not wish to quarrel with this line of reasoning, since I find that this is the way my own personal preferences point.

# ( 8 )

# Amenities and the Law
# of Property

This chapter and the two that follow cover the areas that
have occupied most economists interested in externalities.
Problems of real property are one of the major areas of
orthodox research on externalities. It is also one of the
areas in which governmental action to reduce, or in some
cases to increase, externalities is most common. In one
sense this chapter is unorthodox. I will begin with a rather
conventional presentation of the problem and discussion of
various cures, which is unusual only in that I allot somewhat more space to contractual methods of reducing externalities than is perhaps common. In the latter part of
the chapter, however, I turn to a discussion of the problems raised by governmental decision processes in carrying
out these reforms. These problems tend to be overlooked
or are sometimes simply denounced. For example, in *The
Costs of Economic Growth*, Mishan continuously attacks
the government officials who have caused or permitted

various externalities.[1] Clearly, he does not feel that governmental action is likely to be helpful. In fact, he refers with
apparent disapproval to "pennywise counselors" and suggests as an imaginary alternative an

enlightened municipality which, as a matter of course, sets up
a select committee of citizens, each of which is renowned for
his taste and judgment, charged with the duty of promoting
the beauty and dignity of the city. The principles by which
local authorities and ultimately central government exercise
limited control on building do not correspond with those
proposed here.[2]

We might like to have our affairs managed by enlightened people renowned for their taste, but I do not think
very many of us regard this as a likely outcome. In this
book, I shall discuss the private market as it exists and
governments as they exist.[3] As previously stated, all methods of dealing with externality problems will be imperfect
in one way or another and Mishan, of course, is fully
aware that government action may be inept. For example,
he says, "the cost of intervening and administering a
satisfactory scheme may exceed the apparent social gain." [4]
The principal difference in this respect between my approach and his is that I shall discuss these costs in detail
and he passes over them hastily.

[1] Edward J. Mishan, *The Cost of Economic Growth* (New York:
Frederick A. Praeger, Inc., 1967).

[2] *Ibid.*, pp. 77–78.

[3] In other books I have discussed methods of improving efficiency of
governments. Cf. *The Calculus of Consent* (with James Buchanan) (Ann
Arbor: University of Michigan Press, 1962); *Toward A Mathematics of
Politics* (Ann Arbor: University of Michigan Press, 1966); *The Politics
of Bureaucracy* (Public Affairs Press, 1963). I should say, however, that
although I feel the present governments may be much improved, I doubt
that we will ever achieve Mishan's "ideal city."

[4] Edward J. Mishan, *The Cost of Economic Growth*, p. 55.

A rather special problem that arises when we discuss the externalities connected with real property, or the "amenities" in Mishan's appropriate phrase, is that the reader of this book is probably an intellectual and in the top decile in terms of income. His tastes will normally be quite different from those of the ordinary man. Unfortunately, he is likely to assume that things that disturb him, disturb other people and hence that reduction of externalities will consist largely of changing the world to one that he personally would approve.

Mishan, I would deduce, is somewhat more sensitive than most people to noises.[5] In any event, he continuously refers to various noise problems, such as aircraft flying at their normal operating altitude, and the use of power lawnmowers. I would not wish to deny that these two matters are externalities, but I doubt very much that the average man is deeply concerned with either one. In particular, Mishan's suggestion that overflights be prohibited in certain areas (which would inflict a real and significant cost on air travelers) probably would cause more costs than it would cure. The noise of aircraft taking off is, of course, a different matter.

I also rather suspect that Mishan, who objects to the power lawnmowers run by his neighbor, is creating a negative externality for his neighbor by making the fact that he does object obvious. I suspect, although I must say that I do not know, that he gives visible signs of his impatience and annoyance at this phenomenon. It would seem to me that there is as good an argument for prevent-

[5] In spite of my use of Mishan's book as a whipping boy, it is probably the best general book in its field. It is because it is a superior representation of the general view of the economic community in this area that it is a suitable model for criticisms that are directed at an entire current of thought.

PRACTICE

ing Mishan from expressing annoyance at his neighbor's lawnmower as for preventing his neighbor from running the power lawnmower. But there is a genuine externality. If the small governmental units, which I shall suggest in the latter part of the chapter, existed, I would anticipate (admittedly this is a guess as to other people's tastes) that they would either specify hours in which power mowers can be used or would provide for a joint mowing operation. This solution is suggested by Mishan in his "Pareto Optimality and the Law." [6]

But let us return to the main theme of this chapter and begin by discussing the nature of this type of externality. Let us assume that I own a piece of property next to yours. Under the law, as it exists wherever we are, the ownership of a piece of property means that I can do certain things on that property. What these things are varies from place to place and from time to time. Note, however, that almost anything that I do on my piece of property will have at least some external effects off of it. At the very least, my neighbors will see anything that I do in the open, hear any sounds that I make, smell any odors or smoke that I emit, and suffer danger from any activity I undertake that might cause injury to them.

I could, possibly, take up the manufacture of nitroglycerin as a hobby; beat my wife in public; paint my house an offensive color; run a power lawnmower continuously, or perhaps simply play the trumpet regularly every morning at three o'clock. Turning to external economies; I could plant a beautiful garden, arrange that music that is pleasing to my neighbors regularly emanates from my property, design my house with great care so that it

[6] *Oxford Economic Papers*, 19, no. 3 (Oxford: Clarendon Press, November 1967), 275, footnote 1.

neatly fitted into the general neighborhood, or hire a guard to protect my property who would, by his mere presence, provide at least some protection for my neighbor's property. All of these are externality-generating activities and all are areas in which we would anticipate that a private market would offer a less-than-optimal result.

To some extent, all of these activities are regulated by existing governments. Trumpet playing at three o'clock in the morning would place me in difficulty with the law almost anywhere. Nevertheless, there is no reason to believe that existing regulations are optimal. We must also note that for many of us the regulations are in fact undesirable. It frequently happens, as Mishan points out, that the government officials have rather poor taste, and hence their efforts to improve an area may actually injure it. Still, the fact that present institutions are not perfect is an inconclusive argument for discontinuing them.

Perhaps the most common examples of attempts to reduce externalities are the zoning laws. Although they are not normally discussed in these terms, the zoning laws are basically an effort to reduce the risks associated with owning property. Let us suppose that we lived in a mythical country in which there were no restrictions on what people may do with their property. I am thinking of building a house and I purchase a lot for this purpose. It is possible that the man next door to me will install a drop forge plant, open a bowling alley, begin breeding mosquitoes as a hobby, or perhaps start an explosive manufacturing plant. Clearly, before I purchase my land, I must consider these risks, and the price I would pay for the land would be less than it would be if I knew in advance that the lot next door would have a substantial house built on it.

This line of reasoning seems clear and straightforward,

and most governments have, in fact, accepted it. Laws have been passed making it impossible for me or my neighbor to do certain things on our property and the zoning codes are a collection of such laws. The basic premise of the zoning laws is that individual property owners may be injured by the activity carried on in the adjacent property or in the general vicinity. Consequently, cities are classified into various zones and each type of activity is, generally speaking, restricted to a particular zone. It should be emphasized that this classification is of a peculiar one-way nature in most cases. It is thought, for example, that an apartment building may injure a single-family residential district, but it is not thought that single-family residences will injure apartment buildings. This particular special characteristic of the zoning laws means that you cannot place low-rent apartment buildings in an expensive residential area, but you can build a mansion in a slum area. Needless to say, the wealthy seldom take advantage of this opportunity. The details and precise rules of zoning codes, of course, vary greatly. Furthermore, the specific technique of zoning is essentially an American technique and other methods are used elsewhere.

In theory, there can be no objection to this method of reducing externalities. By reducing the risks that individuals take when they purchase a piece of property, it presumably leads to an increase of total property values and total satisfaction. We are all risk averters. It is notable, in fact, that real estate developers normally impose rules similar to zoning codes on large developments in order to increase the amount of money they can obtain from sales or rentals. Thus, it would appear that this kind of activity can increase the value of land.

In recent years, the question of whether zoning actually

benefits the value of land, and reduces risk has been raised. Otto Davis of Carnegie-Mellon University has written several theoretical pieces indicating that zoning could reduce externalities.[7] Since he was keenly interested in empirical tests, he then proceeded to conduct a statistical study of whether zoning actually reduced undesirable externalities. His tests revealed that there was no such effect.[8] Of the three possible explanations, the one that Davis favors is simply that most people are not really concerned with these externalities. In other words, my willingness to buy a house is not substantially affected by whether or not there is a large apartment house next door. A second possibility is simply that the zoning was poorly conceived. Thus, the benefits of sensible zoning would not appear in the data. The third possibility—that there is something wrong with the rather complicated tests designed by Crecine, Davis, and Jackson—is clearly an open one in spite of the great ingenuity with which these scholars approached their problem. The data were far from ideal, and even the best methods cannot produce more than can be obtained from the data.

Everyone would agree that some uses of land do generate externalities and that regulation may be sensible. The question in most cases, however, is whether the cost of the externality is greater than the cost of eliminating it. Let us, for example, consider Mishan's proposal that automobile traffic be banned in certain areas. In the United States

[7] Otto Davis, "Economic Element in Municipal Zoning Decisions," *Land Economics*, 39 (November 1963): 375–386; and Andrew Whinston and Otto Davis, "The Economics of Complex Systems: The Case of Municipal Zoning," *Kyklos*, 17, no. 3 (1964): 419–445.

[8] John P. Crecine, Otto A. Davis, and John E. Jackson, "Urban Property Markets and Empirical Results and their Implication on Municipal Zoning," *Journal of Law and Economics*, 10 (October 1967): 79–99.

many large tracts of land are being (or have been) developed as new residential areas. The developers can, within fairly wide limits, place any restriction they wish on the use of this land. As far as I am aware, banning automobile travel is unknown in the United States. I would deduce from this that the demand for areas in which automobiles are eliminated is fairly limited.[9]

One does find areas in which automobile traffic is restricted. Many cities have eliminated automobile traffic on streets in the downtown areas in order to improve shopping. Many of the new shopping centers are arranged so that there is an air-conditioned mall for pedestrians. Since these shopping centers, however, were largely developed to make shopping by car convenient and are completely surrounded by gigantic parking lots, this clearly is not an effort to reduce the use of automobiles.

One does, however, not infrequently find cases in which automobiles are restricted to some extent. Directly north of Rice University is a small area that was developed some time ago as an expensive residential subdivision of Rice University. The area owns its own streets, as does Rice University, and has restricted traffic on them to a maximum speed of eight miles per hour. Furthermore, since the street pattern is laid out so that it is impossible to go across the area, an externality is inflicted to some extent on those inhabitants of the city of Houston who do not live in this area. For some trips that they may take, they are required to detour. The property borders heavily traveled roads on three sides and, on the fourth side, is a road of medium-

---

[9] Bermuda has restricted motor vehicles in an effort to promote tourism. It would appear, however, that the vast number of Americans who visit Bermuda enjoy it for a short period of time but would be very distressed if this policy were applied back home.

density traffic. It is probable that, with the exception of the medium-density traffic on the fourth side, these roads would have about the same amount of traffic whether this area restricted traffic or not. It is almost certain, however, that traffic on the fourth side has been increased by the blockage of traffic. Clearly, weighing the costs, few people would object to the inhabitants of the area reducing the externalities that fall on them through traffic and imposing this relatively modest externality on their neighbors.

The problem of noise is extremely complicated. As I have mentioned before, I lived in an apartment house in Houston that offers many services, including rather good sound insulation. Nevertheless, in my apartment I could hear the sirens of ambulances going to and from hospitals, and many ambulances happened to pass close to my apartment building every day. Clearly, this is a negative externality. As it happens, I am not greatly bothered by noise. I know, however, that a number of my neighbors in the apartment building were more sensitive. Furthermore, the sirens were sufficiently loud so that it was practically impossible to deaden their sound by ordinary methods of sound insulation. We could reduce this externality by prohibiting ambulance sirens or requiring the use of less noisy sirens. We do not do so because such regulations would also generate an externality. It would mean that people who are injured would spend longer periods of time getting to the hospital than they do under present circumstances. We thus have an interconnection of two externalities.

There is, however, another problem. Why are the ambulance sirens so loud? The answer appears to be quite simply, and paradoxically, that a great many Americans like quiet. American automobiles are becoming better insulated against sound. The use of heating systems in the winter and air-conditioning in the summer means that automobile windows are very frequently closed. Under the circumstances, a loud siren is necessary to make certain that the automobile drivers hear the ambulance. Thus, the installation of good sound insulation in automobiles makes it necessary for the ambulances to have loud sirens which, in turn, makes the sound insulation in my apartment less efficient. If we compelled automobiles to drive with their windows open, the ambulance sirens could be reduced to a lower level of intensity and hence I would not be disturbed by them in my apartment.

This kind of complex interaction of externalities is common. All one can do in this case is try to offset the different annoyances. Also, as we have mentioned before, there is no obvious reason to believe that the government will choose the optimal offset. In many cases, then, the proper response is to do nothing. If the government intervention is likely to lead to worse results than one would obtain without government intervention, then the fact that the market results are in some sense nonoptimal does not mean that government intervention is called for. Furthermore, to recapitulate what we have said before, if we do decide that government intervention is called for, we must then decide at what level this intervention should be carried out.

But let us return to the procedure we have previously adopted. Let us consider how these externalities may be dealt with by private contract or by government activity. Let us further consider what we can say aout the type of government activity one can hope for. If we concern ourselves with the type of activity that may be undertaken on real property, then it is clear that private contract is sometimes all that is necessary. The developer of a new housing estate, starting with a large plot of land can normally maximize his returns, whether he is renting the land or selling it, by carefully regulating the use to which it is put. The individual purchaser can then consider a great many different sets of such regulations offered by different developers and choose the degree and character of externality regulation that best fits his desires. The system permits people with radically different tastes to obtain their objectives. In other words, by providing plots of land that are large enough so that a great many externalities can be internalized and at the same time small enough so that there is considerable choice available for the individual purchaser, we obtain both a reduction in externalities that are unwanted and the possibility to choose externalities.[10] In those cases in which the individual developer has a plot of land so large that he believes uniform restrictions throughout the plot would not maximize his return, he will divide it into segments and have different restrictions established for each area.

Although the private market works very well in internalizing such externalities, there are two major problems. The first of these arises from what we may call "governmental externalities." The governments in existence in any given area may not permit the individual developers complete freedom in choosing what they wish to do. Let us suppose, for example, that I believe that there is a market for a specialized suburb to be inhabited by people who are consuming marijuana. Clearly, I would simply find myself in prison if I established and widely advertised this com-

[10] This, of course, is subject to the individual's preferences on externalities being sufficiently like those of others so that someone finds it worthwhile providing the service to him. People with highly unusual tastes are unlikely to find either private or government provision very helpful.

munity. On a less conspicuous scale, there are a number of other areas in which I would not be permitted to deviate from the community standards, even if there were a considerable number of people in the community who would be interested in living in such a deviant area.

The second limitation on this private provision of externality-reducing activities is simply that most city property has been broken up into small plots and there is no "owner" who has legal power to decide what the rules shall be for its future use. Indeed, it frequently happens that the developer sells his property, subject to various restrictions, and fifteen or twenty years thereafter these restrictions are no longer desirable. This may be for many reasons, including changing tastes, changing surroundings, technological progress, or simply that the area has "deteriorated." In fact, if we look at most cities, we will observe that the new areas where entrepreneurs are offering specialized combinations of externality-reducing rules are normally only a small part of the total real estate market. This is a consequence of the fact that buildings are long-lasting capital assets, and hence that the new construction is normally a modest part of the total market. For buildings already in existence, this simple procedure of permitting the market to reduce externalities is thus not a very good system.

In this case, we normally turn to governmental restrictions on property. We have mentioned many such restrictions, including the building line and specifications on the type of building. In much of the world, the general architectural appearance of the building will be controlled to make it blend with its neighbors. As another and interesting example, in many cities there are laws requiring that new buildings provide sufficient off-the-street parking.

This is clearly an effort to minimize an externality and could hardly have been put into the deeds many years ago when much of the existing property was originally split up into small units. Furthermore, no individual building owner would be particularly motivated to reduce street congestion because the provision for off-the-street parking for his building would have only a minimal effect.

We have mentioned before that urban renewal has as its principal objective the pooling of divided pieces of land into large tracts in order to internalize externality and make it possible for improvements to be made. In actual practice, urban renewal has not been very successful, but this may be because of inept administration. It may be, of course, that the externalities associated with building lots are not very great. If so, the improvements that can be obtained by controlling the use of land are correspondingly small. It will be recalled that the empirical work done by Crecine, Davis, and Jackson does seem to indicate that the externalities are smaller than would appear to be true from *a priori* reasoning.

Nevertheless, it is clear that there are a great many things that I could do on my property that my neighbors would rather I did not do and that would reduce the value of their land. Laws restricting the use of my property clearly reduce the risk that my neighbors run. In considering the possibility of reducing externalities in real estate, it should be noted that most (although not quite all) of these externalities are of relatively short range effect. As a general rule, I am not likely to be seriously injured by an unsightly building that is more than, let us say, 200 or 300 yards from my lot. In most cases, that building would not even be visible from my property. Thus, this is an area in which the externalities are of relatively short range, and it would seem fairly certain that the optimal way of reducing these externalities would be through a very small governmental agency.

When we turn to this type of activity, however, it may be that the traditional rules of democratic government are not optimal. Experimentation with organizational forms that are different from those to which we are normally accustomed would seem to be called for. It should be noted in this connection that since these areas would be very small, the injury inflicted on any individual through the selection of an inappropriate form of local neighborhood government would normally be modest. It would simply mean that he would have to move and since many people move fairly frequently anyway, the cost would be minimal. There is, in this case, some argument for restricting the franchise to owners of property, provided, of course, that it is a small area and hence that there are a number of competing areas around it. This is because the optimal reduction of externalities will be that which maximizes the value of the real estate. The owners of the real estate would have a clear and unambiguous motive to reach this goal, whereas renters would have other objectives in mind and hence might do a poorer job of reducing externalities. The renters, of course, would be protected from any possible exploitation by the existence of many competing groups of landlords in different areas. Monopoly could cause considerable difficulty.

As I have mentioned before, if small local governmental units were established, which seem to have found favor with many people for a wide variety of reasons, they could deal not only with this type of externality but could also provide certain types of services that local governments characteristically do not now provide. The presumable reason why such governments are not provided today is simply that the local governments are of such a large size that for many citizens the standard services they would provide would be worse than if there were no services at all. Small local areas, however, could provide various levels of services and various levels of taxation. I would anticipate, for example, that a great many such small governments would set up nurseries for the children in their area and, as I have said repeatedly, I think they would take over some gardening from their "taxpayer citizens." But these, of course, are simply guesses on my part as to what would happen; without experimentation we cannot be sure. It is surely true that there are a great many improvements that we can make in the immediate surroundings of our homes. The most efficient way of making these improvements is to have a single landlord owning a fairly large tract of land who considers all of the externalities.[11] This, however, is an impossible objective to achieve in those areas in which the land has already been broken up into small plots. There the establishment of small governmental units having the power to regulate the use of individual plots of land and the general external appearance of the area would probably increase land values through improving living conditions.

[11] He would be in competition with other similar landlords, of course.

# ( 9 )

# Amenities and
# Behavior

Many externalities are not associated with ownership of real estate. An example that obtained a great deal of prominence in Europe three years ago involved many "hippies" who had moved to Rome where they gathered around the Spanish Steps and created a pronounced negative externality for a great many people. Should the Roman police have been encouraged to do what they obviously wanted to do, which was to give the hippies compulsory baths? Should the hippies, on the other hand, have been allowed to continue generating these negative externalities by turning one of the most beautiful spots in Rome into sort of a mobile slum? I can offer my own guess, admittedly no more than a guess, that the injury inflicted on the large collection of tourists and passersby was far greater than the gain to the hippies.[1] If they had been forcibly deported to some relatively undeveloped stretch of beach near

---

[1] The injury inflicted on the police department, who found it necessary to concentrate a fairly large force in the area, must also be considered.

Rome, they probably would have felt almost no reduction in their welfare and a great many people would have felt a distinct improvement.

Many of my readers, however, will feel very strongly that this would not have been desirable. The only reason I can see for objecting would be a distrust of the government. If you feel that government restrictions on appearance, dress, and behavior are apt to be nonoptimal, and in fact will make a bad situation worse, then you would object to government action in this area. There would still be the problem of the boundaries on government control. Practically all governments in the world have some regulations on the clothing and physical appearance of their citizens. This is, of course, because physical appearance does, *ex definition*, generate externalities.[2]

I have discovered that my students are normally deeply shocked when I point out to them that a necktie is worn for the purpose of affecting other people, is a generator of externalities, and hence is a candidate for government regulation. The only point of the necktie from the standpoint of the wearer is the effect the necktie has on other people. In other words, the wearer of the necktie is attempting to affect other people in a way that will to some extent benefit himself. Regardless of their attitude toward regulating the wearing of neckties, however, most people are in agreement with the rules requiring a minimum amount of clothing to be worn in public. Most people also find certain types of attire repulsive, and even if they do not want restrictions on clothing, they do suffer negative externalities from some costumes. The degree to which regulations on clothing are imposed varies widely from society to

[2] J. E. Meade, *Trade and Welfare* (Oxford: Oxford University Press, 1955), p. 20.

society. Sumptuary laws were not historically uncommon, and one of the major features of the recent outburst of juvenile delinquency in China was the imposition of a very stringent set of such laws. We can see an obvious difference between countries that have detailed sumptuary laws and those that do not. The democratic countries in general do not because the individual tends to think of these rules as restricting not only other people's behavior but also his own and has considerable distrust of the government's ability to make optimal rules. Nondemocratic governments are likely to impose such rules because the people running the government think of the rules as controlling other people's clothing and appearance, and have very little distrust of their own efficiency.

One particularly interesting example of the control of clothing is found in countries that require uniforms for students in the lower schools. The normal rationalization for this regulation is that it reduces the degree of inequality in the appearance of the children. Poor children as well as the children of wealthy parents wear the same uniform and, hence, there is very little overt indication of the difference in the status of their parents. Thus, this particular regulation is normally supported on what we may call socially egalitarian grounds. The control of clothing in the English public school was not only socially egalitarian within the school; it also sharply distinguished the students from the unwashed. It is also probable that a mixture of egalitarian motives and desire for a measured degree of inequality provides the rationale for most military uniforms. Uniforms are so widespread today that we tend to forget that they date only from the time of Louis XIV. Although the uniform undoubtedly has use in identifying friends and enemies in close infantry action, most members of the modern armed services are never closely engaged. Thus, requiring them to wear uniforms has no particular utility in terms of identity and must be explained in terms of morale and external effect on others.

One of the considerable number of other types of conduct that we regulate is the making of loud noises in areas in which one does not have property rights. The playing of transistor radios in public has always annoyed me, although it is clear that many people receive positive externalities from their neighbors' radios. Public indecency laws, of course, are an example of efforts to reduce externalities, and so are many laws against what are called public nuisances. In all of these areas, individuals' conduct is controlled. Public drunkenness is another example. I suppose one would list most violations of the traffic codes as examples of individuals inflicting externalities on others by such things as speeding and driving on the wrong side of the road; certainly, illegal parking would be an example. In another book I attempt to develop a large part of the ordinary criminal law out of the economics of externality.[3]

As a general rule, what we have just been discussing is unsuitable for private control. Private individuals can, it is true, establish areas in which certain types of activity are permitted and others are not. The lidos that one finds so commonly on the beaches in Europe are clearly efforts to provide a special environment to customers who wish to go swimming in certain types of surroundings. These surroundings include the behavior of their fellow customers, and, hence, activity is controlled. Restaurants, hotels, and theaters—all regulate the behavior of their customers. Nevertheless, these are privately owned environments, and

[3] Gordon Tullock, *The Logic of the Law: Social Foundations of State-Enforced Norms* (New York: Basic Books, Inc., forthcoming).

PRACTICE

we all must periodically spend a good deal of time in areas that are not private, such as public streets. Here government regulation is clearly necessary.

There is fortunately a fairly simple, although rather rough, rule as to the type of controls on behavior in public places that we should impose. It will be recalled that in earlier chapters we developed the proposition that government action in an area is more likely to be desirable if there is a good deal of uniformity of taste and also, as an independent factor, where the net gain from eliminating the externality is comparatively large. Returning to my example of the neckties, it is perfectly clear that there is very little uniformity in taste in society in this area. It is also quite clear that the elimination of this externality would have only minimal effects on individual welfare, and is thus not a suitable area for regulation. If we turn to the minimum clothing rules, however, we will normally find that the bulk of society agrees that there should be some minimum, although many disagree on what it should be. For a great many people there are very pronounced diseconomies from having this minimum violated. Thus, this would appear to be a case in which regulation would be sensible. Note, however, that the rule we have just proposed is a general one and its application in any given case may be extremely difficult. Nevertheless, I think it will be found that most of the regulations on externality-generating activity in democracies are in cases in which the externality is quite pronounced and where there is a large degree of community consensus. In other words, we have our joint requirement of relatively similar tastes and fairly large costs from externality.

Turning to the type of government unit that is most

192

suitable for dealing with this type of externality, we should begin by observing that, in general, the effect of some type of conduct that generates externalities is fairly short ranged. Both noise and unpleasant sights tend to trail off rapidly as you move away from the point at which they are generated. The same, of course, is true of the positive externalities in this area. Those cities, for example, that maintain public flower gardens or sponsor band concerts for the citizens normally find that the effects of these activities spread only short distances. Here again the externality tapers off quickly, although people may travel a considerable distance for the specific purpose of receiving them.

This would seem to indicate that the restrictions on conduct that may generate externalities should be left to neighborhood governmental units, the very small zones recommended in the last chapter for dealing with the externalities connected with property. In this case, however, there is a countervailing factor. Let us suppose that we permitted numerous very small areas to each specify completely different sets of clothing regulations. Clearly, this would permit a wide diversity of tastes to be maximized, but it would also make it quite difficult for people to move from one of these districts to another. For one thing, people normally literally would not know what the rules were. Property does not move, and the property owners can be expected to learn what the detailed regulations are for each particular piece of property. Rules on conduct deal with a shifting group of people, many of whom will be in a given area for only a short period of time and therefore will not wish to learn a detailed set of restrictions on their behavior. For all of these reasons, it would appear that the optimal area to deal with conduct would be relatively large. We would, of course, still wish to have a number of such different "jurisdictions" in any given area because we would want to satisfy different tastes.

It would be possible for a mixture of a relatively standard set of rules of conduct, together with exceptions for people who feel strongly, to coexist if we permit anyone to do anything on his property provided that it is not visible or audible to his neighbors. If there were large numbers of people in any given area who for one reason or another did not approve of the general rules that had been enacted, it would be possible for them to purchase or rent (or have purchased or rented for them by some person who saw a way of making a profit) a tract of land, and to carry on the type of conduct that they wished within this area. Thus, we could obtain a good deal of variety of activities while at the same time reducing the externalities that may be generated by conduct that violates the aesthetic and ethical norms of the community. If we have a very large number of local government agencies, it would be possible for these agencies to grant exceptions to general "prohibitions." Once again, diversity would be possible in a context of a general rule that reduced externality. The costs of conforming to a general rule would be reduced by this method whereas the externality would, in general, still be small.

The externalities discussed in this chapter have not, in general, received very much analysis from economists. They have also received less analysis from me than have many other subjects. On the whole, it is a sensible allocation of energy. These are not the most important externality effects, yet the fact that these are not the most urgent externalities does not mean that we should pay no attention to them or that we should do nothing to reduce them. In fact, most governments have taken measures to reduce this type of externality and it seems to me that attempting to improve the efficiency of these measures would be sensible.

# ( 10 )

# Common Resources

If the last chapter dealt with externality problems that have not been extensively analyzed by economists, the current chapter will turn to the area that has probably received more economic analysis and more public attention in recent years than any other—the problems of water and air pollution, and the exhaustion (real or imagined) of various resources. As a simple example, I should like to begin with a problem that has, on the whole, avoided solution: the problem of the ownership of an oil pool. Let us suppose that we have a number of farmers living on a piece of land as shown in Figure 12. The boundaries between the farms are shown by the short vertical lines. Someone drills an oil well on one plot of land, shown as A, and finds the oil pool. This is immediately followed by other farmers drilling other wells (I have drawn in one, B). The oil in the pool is a liquid and flows like any other liquid, and hence it is perfectly possible for any individual farmer to draw the oil out from under the land of his neighbor. It is a classic externality.

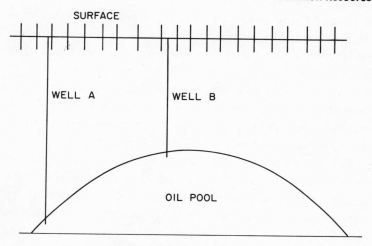

FIGURE 12. An Oil Pool as a Common Resource

In theory one could, of course, compel any given farmer to compensate his neighbor for the oil he has drawn out, but this would require a knowledge of geology that we do not have. If we do nothing at all, it will be foolish for any individual farmer to engage in any conservation since this will mainly benefit his neighbors. Under the circumstances, we would anticipate a rapid drilling of many wells and a rapid exhaustion of the oil pool. We would also anticipate that the technical management of the oil pool would be inept, since it would not be dealt with as a unit. This last factor may mean that the total oil recovery may be as little as 20 per cent of what it could be under a more efficient management.

This scheme is obviously nonoptimal. What we need is some kind of unitized operation of the pool as a whole. In areas in which the land is already divided into small pieces and where land titles extend from "the farthest star to the center of the earth," it is difficult to unitize the pools and, as far as I know practically nothing has been done to solve the problem. The regulatory commissions are more interested in obtaining cartel benefits for the oil producers than in providing for efficient exploitation of the oil. Many of the new oil fields that have been drilled in recent years are located in areas where the land (or sea bottom) held by the individual drilling company is large enough to cover the entire pool and this, of course, obviates the problem.

This is a clear case of a common resource and of sizable externalities. The simplest procedure is to have the entire pool managed as a unit by an organization (such as by compelling the landowners to form a corporation in which each of them holds a number of shares equivalent to the land area he holds over the well, and the corporation operates the field). Another way, at least theoretically, to merge the oil pool would be to work out a system of tax and benefit payments. For example, a special tax could be placed on each barrel of oil drawn up from this well and the returns could be distributed among all landowners over the well. If the tax were properly calculated and varied, it would be possible to obtain exactly the same efficient exploitation as would be obtained by central control.

Most oil experts tend to believe, however, that unitizing the pool under one management is the simple way of dealing with the problem. There are other exhaustible resources in which this is not so. Let us consider the fisheries. The more I fish, the fewer fish are left for you to catch. If many fishermen are engaged in fishing in a given area, the net return may not be markedly higher, or in fact over a period of time it may be much lower than if the number of fishermen were limited. This externality is characteristically dealt with through a fantastically inefficient scheme. The government restricts fishing either in time or as to the methods that are used in such a way as to run up the costs to individual fishers, which means that the most efficient techniques are banned and there is a great overinvestment in fishing. The simple procedure would be to impose a tax on fish landed that reflected the externality. Unfortunately, this simple, straightforward technique of dealing with the fisheries has not been adopted anywhere except by private owners of a few lakes and streams, which is particularly surprising since such a tax surely would bring in a fair amount of revenue.

Another common resource (one that we have mentioned previously) is the street and highway system. This is a fairly clear-cut case in which individual decisions, that is, decisions to use a highway during a rush hour, inflict sizable costs on other people. Once again, there are a number of ways of dealing with the problem, but the most efficient would appear to be charging a high price for use of the highway during periods of congestion.

But these are merely a small sample of the cases in which resources, instead of being divided up among individual persons, may be used by anyone. For much of human history, many pastoral tribes owned their pastures in common, that is, the individual owned the sheep, goats, and cattle, but the land they grazed was held in common. No individual had any motive to adjust the number of cattle he held to the land on which it was grazing. It led to what is known as overgrazing, and the total number of cattle was substantially lower than could have been maintained by a more efficient allocation of grazing. The American Old West was an example of this phenomenon, and fencing certainly led to an increase in cattle production.

It has been widely argued (although the matter is still

extremely controversial) that the "property ownership" of so many species of birds and animals is an evolutionary method of reducing overgrazing and, hence, permits a larger number of members of the species to survive. Unfortunately, the biological evidence is extremely difficult on this point, but we can say that there is nothing economically improbable about the hypothesis.[1] If the birds and many of the animals have private property of this sort, then we can say that many primitive human tribes have actually retrogressed from the state of their animal ancestors. Of course, there are many animals in which the property concept seems to apply to a tribe rather than to an individual or family, and it may well be that our ancestors came from that type of an animal society.

Recent concern with air and water pollution is yet another example of a natural resource used in such a way as to reduce its value. The atmosphere, for example, is a common resource used by all. It has the ability to absorb a great many things that may be dumped into it. Every person reading this book, for example, is dumping carbon dioxide and certain other body wastes into the air simply because he is breathing. Furthermore, we all make use of the resource for the oxygen that we need to live and for certain other things such as a clear medium for vision.[2] The more debris we dump into the air, particularly auto-

[1] For presentation of the two sides of the debate, see Robert Andrey, *The Territorial Imperative* (New York: Atheneum Publishers, 1966), and David Lack, *Population Studies of Birds* (Oxford: Clarendon Press, 1966).

[2] In this case, it would appear that the famous pea-soup fogs of London were almost entirely caused by air pollution via the use of soft coal. With the movement toward other methods of heating, London continues to be foggy but no longer does it have extraordinary dense fogs. This is, of course, a case in which an externality was greatly reduced simply by technological progress.

mobile exhaust, the less suitable the air becomes for other uses. Places such as Los Angeles are, of course, extreme examples. I, myself, acquired sinus difficulty by spending two months in Los Angeles.

The problem is that the individual, in producing automobile exhaust, smoke, or his own breath does not consider the effect that this emission will have on other people. The atmosphere is capable of absorbing a large amount of such debris, and until recently the volume that it was capable of absorbing was (except perhaps in London) so great that no one noticed that the air was becoming somewhat less clean. With the progress of civilization and the much greater use of energy, we have now begun to dump large enough amounts of debris into the air so that it has become highly noticeable.

As my example, may I take one that as far as I know has never been previously discussed and (since I have not made calculations) may, in fact, be trivial. Nevertheless, it is an interesting example and it seems to me it might be worthy of an engineering study. It concerns air-conditioning in large cities. An air-conditioning unit removes heat from an enclosed space and transfers it to the outside. Furthermore, the operation of the air-conditioning unit generates a good deal more heat. Thus, it is certainly true that the outside air temperature in New York City is higher as a result of air-conditioning than it otherwise would be. The only problem here is whether this effect is large enough to worry about. For purposes of analysis, we can discuss the matter without raising the particular problem of whether the effect is or is not very large.

Clearly, in this case, the cost of air-conditioning a room is higher if other people are using air-conditioners in the vicinity because the outside air temperature will be higher.

Perhaps more important, people who are not at the moment in an air-conditioned space will find that the air is hotter and hence more uncomfortable. In both cases, the cooling of the air-conditioned space is partially offset by the warming of other space. Optimization would require that individuals be somehow compelled to take this fact into account. Economists would recommend a tax on air-conditioning. The problem, from the standpoint of conventional economics, appears to be fairly simple, although the technology may, of course, be highly complicated. This is particularly true in the case of air pollution, since although automobile exhaust is overwhelmingly the largest source of air pollution, the interaction of different types of gases and dust in the air is quite complicated, and it may be that the simple measure of the amount of pollution caused by one source is quite difficult.

Water pollution presents a roughly similar problem. Many people, through the domestic sewage system and industry, dump waste into water courses. It is, in fact, one of the cheapest ways of getting rid of such things as sewage and industrial waste. The waters of the world are capable of accepting a good deal of such pollution without damage. In fact, natural water courses are frequently extremely polluted. There are natural bodies of water in which no fish can live and anybody who has seen the Mississippi and remembers that its Indian name means "big muddy" will realize that the contamination of water is not solely a human enterprise. Furthermore, there is no reason why we should try to make the water in all streams chemically pure. I recently read a proposal for requiring that all companies who place water in streams make certain that the water is as pure as is technically possible. This would require that the companies engage in multiple distilling operations and produce water that is much purer than the water they receive from the city water services.

Actually it is likely that individually produced wastes in the form of the run-off of water over plowed farmland and sewage are the major offenders in the United States. There are areas, of course, where this is not the case, and it is certainly true that many industrial plants dump unpleasant products into the water. Once again the simple solution would appear to be a suitable tax on the people who place pollutants into water both in order to derive some revenue and to obtain optimal internalization of the externalities. Although there are technical problems in calculating the optimal tax, it does not appear to be difficult to obtain an approximation. The problems are essentially matters of chemistry and engineering. In this area, we have one highly successful organization that deals with the problem by a method of taxes and subsidies: the Ruhr consortium, which has been so well described by Allen Kneese.[3]

Although the economics seem fairly simple, anyone who has paid any attention to the controversies surrounding these matters is aware that our political mechanisms seem to be poorly adapted to solving the problems. The Ruhr consortium is a unique institution. Almost everywhere else the governmental agencies either ignore real problems or adopt inappropriate remedies.

Two examples may help. First, for some time I had as a graduate student a professional economist employed by the Department of Interior to work on externality problems. In the course of one of the number of discussions I had with him on the subject, he remarked that every econ-

---

[3] Allen Kneese, *Water Pollution: Economic Aspects and Research Needs* (Baltimore: Johns Hopkins University Press, 1962).

omist who had ever studied the problem had rapidly come to the conclusion that taxes or perhaps taxes and subsidies were the optimal solution. He also remarked, however, that no political leader would accept that solution. The politicians characteristically wanted a flat law limiting the amount of pollution. This is inherently inefficient since it does not permit the type of adjustment under which those plants that can reduce pollution cheaply do a great deal of it and those plants in which reduction is very expensive are permitted to produce more pollution.

His observation of the real world is surely accurate. We find few cases of political discussions of externality that even mention the possibility of taxes. The problem is always said to be one of "setting standards." Furthermore, these "standards" are normally set in a most peculiar way. Instead of attempting to compute the injuries that may be inflicted by placing pollution in water or air or by causing congestion, and offsetting this against the cost of eliminating such pollution, the usual procedure is to treat pollution as an infinite evil. Clearly, this is not true and the practical politicians, as opposed to the ideologists, usually try to find an absolute rate of pollution that is a compromise between those who want no pollution and the businessmen who would like to have low costs.

These compromises have, as far as I know, never been the result of any significant economic calculation. I must admit, however, that I may be overlooking some examples. Still, the general impression one gets from reading newspapers is that the pollution problem is being dealt with in an extraordinarily inept way. There does not seem to be any reason to believe that any of the regulations are even close to being optimal. Whether the antipollution restrictions we now have are better or worse than no restriction at all is a question that I have no way of answering. I suspect that they do represent an improvement over a policy of *laissez faire*, but the improvement clearly is modest compared to what could be done. So much for my first example. My second example concerns the largest single producer of air pollution: automobile exhaust. Automobile exhaust is unique in that it is not only a major source of contaminants but it also does not significantly reduce the purity of the air in most parts of the country. The number of automobiles operating is small compared to the cubic space of air above them and, hence, except in a few large cities, the automobile exhaust is diluted to the point where it has no deleterious effect.

However, in large cities this is not true. Under these circumstances, it seems clear that the appropriate restriction on automobile exhaust would be to strictly regulate it in large cities where it is a special problem, Los Angeles for example, and leave it substantially unregulated everywhere else. It is notable that this particular proposal does not seem to have much political appeal. Efforts in Los Angeles itself to compel drivers in the city to install devices that would reduce the output of pollution were extremely difficult to institute, mainly because it appears that the bulk of the voters objected to them. The history of the eventual adoption of laws on this subject in Los Angeles is almost identical to that which one would anticipate if some minority that happened to contain most of the intellectuals was attempting to get special interest legislation. Once the legislation was enacted, the citizens of Los Angeles rapidly developed methods of evading performance and the police force made no particular effort to enforce the law.

There are several possible explanations for this disap-

PRACTICE

pointing performance. The first is simply that the average individual may not have believed the technical evidence indicating that the smog in Los Angeles was largely caused by automobile exhaust. A second may be that, although the average individual did indeed object to smog, his objection to smog was less than his objection to the cost of eliminating it. If this second explanation is true, then, of course, the institution of costly devices for reducing exhaust was noneconomic and should not have been undertaken.

The eventual "solution" has been the enaction of national legislation requiring that all new cars be equipped in such a way as to reduce the amount of pollution released from their exhaust. This solution is extremely wasteful since there is no reason why most cars operating in the United States should have this equipment and it is also a poor way of dealing with the problem in such places as Los Angeles. If people were serious about wanting to get this type of pollution reduced, it would be desirable to have all cars, not simply that portion which are new, equipped with exhaust-purifying devices. Once again, the outcome seems rather like a compromise between a small special interest group worried about pollution and the general public that is not.

For another example of the ineptness with which our governments have normally dealt with these problems, we can turn to the oil pools that I discussed at the beginning of this chapter. In California, it was proposed that all such pools be compulsorily unitized by state action. This led to a vigorous political campaign and defeat of the measure by public referendum, a clear-cut case in which the voters voted against an externality-reducing change in institutions. It is particularly impressive because, of course, the

206

average voter was not directly concerned with this particular externality.

In some externalities it is possible to specify an optimal area to make the decisions on internalizing these externalities. The city of Houston and its suburbs, for example, has an air-pollution problem, caused probably by the automobile exhaust of Houston, but it may also be a result of the refining industry.[4] Clearly, this is the type of pollution that can be fairly readily dealt with by the local community. The surrounding ranch land is not significantly injured by the pollution, and therefore there is a fairly well-defined area within which the pollution is injurious. The area around Los Angeles would provide another area as probably would the area around New York City. The oil pools, of course, can be fairly readily defined, and most water pollution problems concern particular water courses. Hence the optimal operation unit would be the water course basin, which is the way the Ruhr River is operated.

Unfortunately, there are other externalities in which the problem is not so simple. As a general rule, air pollution declines as the square of the distance from the source. Thus, instead of having a point at which pollution stops, one has a gradual decline of the pollution. This makes it extremely difficult to say what is the optimal area for dealing with such externalities.

Even if we could determine the optimal area, there seems to be no very strong reason to believe that any governmental agency would be motivated to enact the optimal institution, whatever it is. In this area there have been

---

[4] It is indicative of the general lack of public interest in a scientific approach to pollution problems that, although most of my friends at Rice University talked a great deal about air pollution in Houston, none of them bothered to inform themselves of the source of the pollution.

many computations by economists and engineers that indicate that large savings can be made. As a general rule, these computations involve a certain number of arbitrary assumptions, but I think we can give a good deal of respect to them while hoping that, as time proceeds, they will be improved. Suppose, however, we were able to compute an optimal degree of air pollution in the form, let us say, of a tax in Houston. Is there any obvious reason why the political leaders of Houston would be pressed by the voters to enact this tax? I have been unable to design any voting procedure that has even a modest tendency to produce the optimal outcome. Thus, it would seem likely that politicians will normally adopt inappropriate means for dealing with these externalities. If we observe the real world, we observe that this hypothesis is verified. There are very, very few governmental agencies that have achieved an optimal, or even close to optimal, degree of reduction of externalities. It does not, of course, follow that we should do nothing or that the government should refrain from involvement in such areas as air and water pollution. What it does indicate is that we should not anticipate that government "reforms" in these areas will be ideal. We should recognize that the government intervention will probably be inept, and hence restrict it to those areas where the private externality costs are large.

There is, however, one possible method by which the government might deal with these problems in a more efficient manner. The reader's attitude toward this method is apt to be highly correlated with his view about civil servants and economists, and I thus offer it only as a tentative suggestion. The legislature could enact a bill setting up an engineering and economic computing center, which, with respect to any particular externality, could apply the best methods available to determine what is the optimal amount of tax and subsidy to reduce the externality. It could then provide that whatever decision was produced by the technicians would automatically become law without further legislative action. Since this bill would deal with a very large number of future decisions, an individual could expect to be a beneficiary in the future more often than a victim, simply because the total benefits would be greater than the total injury.

It is not impossible that a legislature might be convinced that this type of bill would be desirable. As we have stated, computations in this area, although clearly subject to great improvement, are nevertheless worthy of a good deal of respect now. It seems likely that this institution, if the economists and civil servants carried out their instructions, would reduce externality costs. As I have stated previously, I suspect that whether people will favor it or not will depend very largely on their attitude toward giving this kind of power to a nonelected body.

In any event, the problems of dealing with common resources to which this chapter has been devoted are technically not terribly difficult. A great deal more research is, of course, necessary, but in general we have a fairly good idea of what we want. The problems that we face in this area are designing governmental agencies so that the technically optimal measures are likely to be approximated. Thus far, we have made substantially no progress in this field.

# ( 11 )

# Protection

The name Paul Samuelson is inextricably connected with the subject of "public goods." Since Samuelson clearly had a tremendous influence in the development of this field, it may seem ungracious if this chapter does not follow his approach. The approach used by Samuelson was a great step forward at the time, but by now most of the advantages from this approach have been gained, and it has been discovered that it does have some disadvantages. Thus, I approach the matter in a slightly different way with the objective of obtaining all of the advantages of Samuelson's work and eliminating the (rather minor) defects.

In a number of traditional governmental activities there are very great economies if the service is provided throughout a large, contiguous area. As examples, we may mention the defense of the country, its foreign policy, the policing of the country, the provision of a legal system, and control of contagious diseases.[1] This list is not, of course, exhaus-

---

[1] The development of modern antibiotics has greatly reduced the importance of contagious disease. As recently as my childhood, however, control of contagion was an important government function.

tive, but it does provide us with enough to consider for the moment.

If we consider defense against people who might be interested in stealing our property or perhaps committing physical violence upon us, and temporarily assume that these people are not organized in large units, then the traditional defense unit is the police force. The police make use of basically two techniques: patrolling areas in order to prevent crimes from occurring, and arresting people after crimes have been committed in order to make the present discounted value of a crime negative because the probability of an unpleasant outcome is high enough to more than counterbalance the profit that may be made from the commission of the crime. We may divide these two activities roughly into "patrol" and "detection."

The second of these two activities (detection) does not seem to require contiguous areas. In the United States and in other countries, there are large private detective forces which operate on discontiguous property. Most insurance companies, for example, maintain detective divisions that investigate cases in which the insurance company suffers a loss and in which it is felt that the use of additional resources may result in reduction of losses. There are also a number of private detective agencies that contract with individual businesses for additional protection. The detective agency supplements the regular police force by attempting to capture a person who commits a crime on the protected property. Apparently the net effect of this is regarded as positive by a great many businessmen, because many of them have purchased such service.

An examination of the work of detectives, then, seems to indicate that the problems of contiguity are not very important in their area. They deal with specific crimes and are seldom interested in the place the crime is committed except insofar as there may be jurisdictional problems, which could be readily dealt with by any one of a large number of techniques. It may be, however, that the detectives create a significant externality. The arrest and jailing of a burglar may offer protection not only for the people who hired the detectives but for other people as well. If this is so, it would be desirable that this externality be internalized. In practice, of course, the government maintains a force of detectives engaged in attempting to solve crimes. Since there may be externalities, this is not necessarily an inefficient procedure, but it seems likely that the reason why we have these detective forces is not that they are efficient, but that they were an outgrowth of the patrolling part of the police function.

Patrolling produces large externalities. If I hired a patrolman to stand in front of my property for short, randomly selected, periods of time, he would have to pass by a number of pieces of property in order to reach mine. Thus he would automatically provide protection for the property of others. It would be irrational for any individual to contribute to the pay of the policeman if he could avoid it. Thus we have a situation in which all of us join together and agree to force ourselves to pay to hire a policeman. This is an extreme case of an externality.

It should be noted, however, that the externality of the patrol function of the police department seems to be geographically limited. Small police departments seem to function efficiently. In general, it would appear that a half square mile or so is all that is necessary for internalizing patrol externalities. If the patrol function of the police department were broken up into small units, patrolling would occur at different levels of density and quality in different areas. This should lead to a higher net efficiency of the employment of resources. It is, of course, true that the centralized police forces do not patrol everywhere equally, but their arrangements for varying the density of their patrol is presumably less desirable than that which could be obtained if residents of each small neighborhood determined how heavily their area would be patrolled.

There are apparently some scale economies in providing police patrol forces, but this does not require any very large governmental unit. It is possible to subcontract patrol either from a government agency, as it is widely done by small cities in Los Angeles County, or from private sources (a new and burgeoning industry).

The difference between police activities and national defense is not as large as one might think. It is reported that a pirate captured by Alexander the Great told the king that the only difference between them was the number of ships under their command. There is much in this comment. The use of force to compel transfers is an old and established human custom. The real difference between the problems of national defense and the problems of ordinary crime is simply a matter of scale. The Mafia, in a way, is an intermediate case. If, for example, the Germans had won the last war, they would (I feel sure) be now obtaining a very considerable income from their French and Russian possessions. The Russians, in fact, received a magnificent return from their conquest of Eastern Europe, which was obtained by threat of or, occasionally by, the use of force. A conqueror would attempt to minimize private burglary, since it would reduce the returns on his holdings. It should be noted that well-organized extortion gangs who use the threat of violence to obtain a tax from people living in certain of our less well policed cities, also avoid such simple crimes as burglary. If you are able to obtain a position of power, then the simple use of power to extort funds is efficient.

The problem here is simply that in the use of violence, there are large scale economies. The individual may be able to protect himself against any other individual but not against a group of them. In general, the larger the group, the more likely it is to win. "God is on the side of the big battalions." One hundred thousand people can obtain more effective defense by grouping together into one large unit than by acting as a number of small units. This is the real reason that the major states exist and the reason that we refer to great and small powers.

Thus, in protecting ourselves against the seizure of our property and perhaps injury of our persons by those large organized bands that we call armies, we depend on economies of scale. Small countries could, and historically frequently did, simply hire large armies at times of difficulty, thus avoiding the costs of continuously maintaining armies. Such hired armies may, however, suggest that their salaries be raised. Furthermore, in general, a small country simply cannot afford to hire a large army. It would find it necessary to have allies in order to retain its independence.

Once again, however, we have our problem of contiguity. The defense of an area is normally simpler if it is relatively compact. A corporation that attempted to sell "national defense" to a number of customers who were not located so that their properties were contiguous would find the costs were gigantic compared to the costs of protecting a similar number of customers whose property was contiguous. Hence, once more we have an area in which government action is desirable and in which it would appear that the larger the unit, the better would be the results.

The point, to repeat, is that the production of military force, or for that matter violence of any sort, is subject to very great economies of scale. This is perhaps best illustrated in the traditional military rule that when two forces meet, the probability of victory is proportional not to the ratio of their strengths, but rather to that of the squares of their strengths.

This being so, economists would anticipate that individual countries would grow until a single military force covered the entire world. Every time that two countries were combined, whether by conquest or by any other method, they would by that simple act acquire a disproportionate increase in military force and hence would be able to conquer other countries. It is the situation of production under declining costs so familiar to economists, and the theorem that as long as costs of production continue to decline, there is no way of preventing a movement to monopoly, would at first glance appear to apply.

There is another potentially great economy if the world were brought under the control of the same monopoly of force. The size of the force needed to control the world would be smaller than the total size that would be needed for any significant portion of the world simply because there would be no organized enemy. We have a rather neat illustration of this in a situation that occurred after India was "freed and partitioned." The English had been able to defend India without any real difficulty with a relatively small army. The two nations, which shared the Indian peninsula after the partition, rapidly found it necessary to increase their military budgets mainly to build armies against each other. Military appropriations rose to a vastly larger figure than under the Raj. The fact that these countries chose independence with heavy military burdens to incorporation within a powerful empire with the accompanying economies of scale is evidence that there must be some counterbalancing factor.

Let us, however, leave that subject for later discussion and point out now that history does reveal a large number of cases in which the process we have been describing has occurred. At one time, the Mediterranean basin was divided among five powerful nations: Rome, Carthage, Ptolemaic Egypt, Antigonid Macedonia, and Selucid Syria. The Selucid Empire extended, of course, far beyond the Mediterranean. There were also a number of smaller countries. Rome won battles, used these conquests to support larger military forces, and thus was able to win more battles, and eventually brought peace to the entire area. The same history has been repeated in various parts of the world many, many times, of which Chin Shih Huangti's pacification of China serves as a further example. The outthrust of the Mohammedan armies from the Arabian desert is another example, and the development of the Mongolian Empire is perhaps the best example of all. In the past, these vast military aggregations never controlled the entire world, but this simply reflects the former technological limitations on long distance movement.

Nevertheless, although we clearly can comprehend this particular economic argument for very large armies, for the big fish swallowing the small fish, we also observe the opposite phenomenon. In recent years a large number of the people in the world have chosen to move from being defended by a powerful military machine to being tiny, helpless countries. The Algerians, for example, fought hard in order to deprive themselves of efficient military protection. They now find that they must make vast expenditures for much less protection against foreign enemies than France could readily have given them. Nevertheless, they seem satisfied with the exchange.

The problem, of course, is that people have different desires, and they may prefer a situation in which the people making decisions (whether dictators as in Algeria or democratically elected officials as in Israel) are more closely related to them than is the case in a world empire. They are willing to take their chances with an inferior military position for this end. As a simple example, consider Israel. Israel is in a very difficult military situation and finds it necessary to expend large resources in dealing with that military situation. Furthermore, she finds it necessary to regularly defy the United Nations, something that I think most Israelis find painful. Let us suppose that President Nasser, noting this fact and noting also that clearly the economies of scale would indicate that combined military forces of Egypt and Israel could do a much better job of defense than either of them could as independent armies, were to suggest to the Israeli government that the two countries combine. He is, of course, a dictator, but I think he could safely suggest a democracy with one-man-one-vote. The Israelis would surely reject this proposal, in fact they would regard it as absurd. The reason is simple. They prefer their present perilous military situation to simple majority voting in a constituency in which they themselves are a minority.

There is no reason why we should criticize the Israelis for this attitude. We could, I think, have obtained a very efficient military protection for ourselves if we had, let us say in 1937, surrendered totally to Hitler. Today we could obtain great military security in the sense of a highly efficient military machine if we were to quickly surrender to the Russians. In both cases, of course, we would have to take the initiative in the absence of active war, but if we were simply interested in obtaining efficient organization of the use of force, this would be the way to do it. The absurdity of the proposal illustrates that we would rather have our preferences implemented even if the cost is a less-than-optimality provision of military resources. The colonial countries who have recently achieved their independence are simply extreme examples of this phenomenon.

There is nothing to be surprised about here. We have, from the beginning, pointed out that externalities must be set off against the desirability of having the governmental unit adjust to individual preferences. It is clear that the best mix can be obtained in most countries by maintaining a national rather than a global defense system. There is, of course, no reason to believe that the present units are optimal in this regard, but there is also no reason to be confident that any particular change would be an improvement.

The traditional techniques of alliances, leagues, and federations are efforts (not terribly successful efforts) to combine the advantages of small internal decision-making units with the military advantages of large scale. It is possible that with ingenuity something along these lines could be developed that would be a great improvement over our present mix of state sizes. As one who has thought a great deal about foreign policy, I can only say that this is a possibility. None of the concrete proposals that I have heard suggested or that I have been able to think of myself is likely to work.

I would suggest that a number of countries whose cultural similarities are strong—the Spanish, the Arab countries, or the English-speaking countries—might combine into a unit having only military and foreign policy responsibilities. Presumably it would be sensible to have free trade within the organization, some kind of central governmental organization suitable for a very restricted set of tasks, and probably a single very simple form of revenue, such as the value added tax. But this is obviously merely a suggestion serving in the way of example. It may be that there is nothing we can do to improve the present situation. Research is the standard answer of any scholar to any problem, and I am afraid that I must suggest it here.

Turning now to other matters, one of the functions of most governments is the maintenance of a legal system. By this, I do not mean that part of the legal system that works with the police department to maintain domestic peace. Criminal courts, as a result of historical accident, are completely separate from the police in most Western states. The courts however, are simply a sort of review process for police activities. In many parts of the world, in fact, they are incorporated in the police force. Most of the Communist countries, until very recently, imprisoned people by a decision of a middle-grade police officer, or in some cases a committee of middle-grade police officers. I do not like to cite this as an example of desirable practice, but it is fairly clear that the appalling nature of Communist control methods were not much affected by this institution. In the American Old West, once again, as a result of a series of rather odd accidents, there was also a melding of the police and the judiciary The police were United States Marshals and the local judge was the superior of the marshals. As far as I know, we have never had any reason to regard the output of this particular system in which the judiciary and the police force were combined as being inferior to the present system. This, however, has been a digression. The point that I am now making is that the establishment by the state of a set of courts that will enforce contracts if the parties wish and are available to deal with personal injury cases, and such matters as violation of minor, non-criminal statutes is an important governmental function. Indeed the modern economy could not function without it, and most people will agree it is desirable. Since I have written another book on this general subject, I will not discuss it in detail.[2]

The intriguing feature, however, is that it would appear to be a case in which externalities are of only limited scope. The English use a system in which a large portion of the lower judiciary is composed of amateurs. Furthermore, in many parts of the United States the small towns have their own part-time judge, which again seems to work reasonably well. It would thus seem that we could operate a court system of part-time judges in certain relatively small areas. Perhaps this would not be the most efficient system, but we need further research before we can say that larger units are desirable. Thus, this particular activity probably could be carried on by relatively small governmental units. We do not, unfortunately, have enough data on the efficiency to be sure about the optimum, but there is certainly no reason to believe that anything such as a nationwide organization is necessary. In the United States, of course, almost all judicial activity is operated on a state and local level. The federal court system, although it deals with a number of important cases, deals with but a tiny fraction of the total.

The public road system is a further example of a "public good." It seems to be impossible to design competing road systems, although one can well imagine competing

---

[2] Gordon Tullock, *The Logic of the Law: Social Foundations of State-Enforced Norms* (New York: Basic Books, Inc., forthcoming).

turnpikes. In fact, we have developed something similar to this in certain areas, but it is difficult to imagine how competing roads could reach each house in the city or each farm in the country because of the impossibility of two roads occupying the same space. Under the circumstances, a private entrepreneur who owned the roads would have a monstrous monopoly. Not only would he have the right to charge for normal use of the roads, but since it would be impossible to move very far without crossing one of his roads, he could obtain substantially the entire rent of any property.

Granted that it is impossible to produce a competitive road network, and the importance of the roads both as a means of transportation and as (in essence) pieces of real estate that enclose all other pieces of real estate, government control seems reasonable. There is no reason why we should object to any private person who wishes to put up a competing road, but I doubt that there will be many who wish to take advantage of this opportunity.[3]

Here, however, we have problems in selecting the unit of government and the way in which it shall pay for transportation. It is arguable that transportation should be paid for entirely by taxes collected on vehicles. The gasoline tax, of course, is a step in this direction, although it is far from an ideal tax.[4] The second problem dealing with the taxes required for automobiles is one we have discussed previously, the problem of congestion, which would seem to indicate that different prices should be used for different

[3] For many years there was a private motor road running out to Long Island from New York.

[4] The problem with the gasoline tax as presently collected is that it leads to trucks being underpowered, with the result that they are a traffic hazard. Presumably, this could be eliminated, but present institutions are suboptimal.

roads and for that matter at different times. This is technically feasible in this day of computers, but little action has been taken.

So much for the tax problem. The unit to control the highways is a difficult problem. An improved highway mainly benefits people who are driving short distances on that highway. It benefits to a lesser extent, however, people who are making long trips in which part of that highway is involved; and finally it probably benefits people who live as far away as Australia in that some of the merchandise carried on the highway will have its price lowered.

The solution that is actually used to deal with this problem involves dividing the responsibility of highway maintenance and construction among a number of levels of government. This division can be extremely detailed. In the town in which I was raised, Rockford, Illinois, the decision of whether or not to have curbs on a street was made by the householders on each individual block. They would hold a small election and if they voted to have the curb installed, the city would do the construction and then charge the householders. This system is also used in some American cities for the paving of local streets. On the other hand, larger governmental units normally deal with other parts of the transportation network. This can be done by dividing the highway network into local roads and major roads and having the central government deal with the major roads and the local government pay for local roads. Another method involves local government control of roads supplemented by central governmental subsidies.

As a final example of a public good, let us consider the control of contagious diseases, once a major problem, and even today still one of some importance. In this case, the government, in order to control contagion, places restrictions on the freedom of movement of certain members of society. These restrictions may be no more than a requirement that a person not cross the national boundary unless he has a smallpox inoculation. Quarantines preventing a contagious person from having contact with the rest of the population are largely a thing of the past today. The prevention of the spread of agricultural pests, however, is still mainly dependent upon similar regulations.

Here we have a clear case in which the externalities can be quite large and in which the cost of reducing them by governmental action is quite low. It is very hard to see any way in which private persons could undertake this type of activity with anything even closely approximating the economy that is available for the government. But note again that it is a matter of the technology. Prevention of contagion was an important governmental activity not very long ago, but today it is trivial.

# ( 12 )

# Production of
# Knowledge

The four previous chapters have been devoted to discussing areas in which the externality problem has attracted a good deal of attention by economists. The following three chapters are devoted to the discussion of areas of equal importance, but those in which relatively little research has been carried out. This chapter deals with the problem of research, which is frequently used in discussions of externality as an example of an externality-producing activity, but seldom analyzed in any detail. The following two chapters deal, respectively, with the flow of information, a subject that has almost never been analyzed in externality terms, and income redistribution, which is only occasionally discussed in these terms.

In regard to research, production of new knowledge is an almost perfect illustration of an externality-generating activity. If I discover something, say a cure for cancer, then anyone who knows of this discovery can use it. The number of beneficiaries is almost certain to be vastly greater than the number of people who contributed to providing the new information. Furthermore, the cure is an example of a "public good," that is, the addition of one more consumer does not change the cost. The use of the new knowledge by other persons does not increase the cost of production.[1]

Present-day society offers two ways of encouraging the production of new knowledge. The first of these is to give the person who produces the new knowledge a property right to it, in the form of a patent. The patent, which permits the individual to charge a price for the use of the knowledge, has been the subject of considerable economic controversy for a long time. I do not wish to enter into the controversy and will simply point out that this method does, indeed, encourage the production of new knowledge in those areas in which it is applicable. The question of whether the patent system encourages production to the optimal amount is difficult to answer. If I avoid the subject, it is not that I think that the present institutions are ideal, but that I think I have little to contribute. Instead, I should like to turn to that type of knowledge that is not patentable.

There are many areas in which it would be desirable to increase knowledge and in which patents are not possible. In some instances, the legal system simply does not permit patents, although in some sense it "should." The refusal of the Italian government to grant patents on new drugs is an example of this. Fortunately, this refusal has not greatly retarded the research in the development of new medicines because the Italian drug market is far from large. It has,

---

[1] Although the knowledge itself is a public good, it should be noted that the dissemination of the knowledge may not be. In fact, it may be extremely costly to acquire knowledge of new developments, and this may be a completely private cost.

however, reduced the amount of research on new drugs in Italy to some extent.

There are, however, many areas in which a patent is not even theoretically possible. An invention of a new sales technique, for example, would not be patentable because it would be extremely difficult to tell what people were making use of it. Similarly, a great many (although not all) of the improvements in the technology of agriculture involve simple changes in the method by which certain things are done by the farmer. These changes are not patentable because it would be impossible to police the countryside and prevent farmers who had not paid the fees for planting their corn [let us say] six-and-one-quarter inches apart. The same is true for many production routines and management techniques in factories. Turning from these cases of straightforward efforts to improve mechanical efficiency to what we normally call pure research, that is, an effort to increase knowledge without any clear idea as to how the increase in knowledge will be used. It has two positive effects; the first of these is to satisfy curiosity. We would like to know what the other side of the moon looks like. The second of these effects is that such discoveries may, in the future, lead to improved technology of some sort.

Clearly, if the new knowledge is worth anything, it is as a generator of externalities. In fact, the scope of these externalities is (roughly speaking) the solar system. It is not possible to tell who will find this information either entertaining or positively useful. Thus, we deduce that the average person would find some type of subsidization of research a desirable governmental activity. Furthermore, we could deduce that this subsidization would be on an international scale, since only in this way can we internalize all externalities. Unfortunately, the problem is more complex. Although the externalities in this case do not adhere to any particular geographic location, it is nevertheless probably true that the subsidization through international agencies would be less efficient than it would be by the smaller units that now exist.[2] This is not, of course, because the externalities in this case are small.

The history of science seems to indicate that it is highly undesirable for the financial support of science to be centralized. The man who has a new and revolutionary idea should not be placed in the position in which one organization or board can say no. He should be provided with a number of alternative sources of support so that the new idea is more likely to escape simple prejudice. Thus, even within national boundaries, it seems that it would (on the whole) be desirable to have the provision of subsidy for scientific work decentralized.

Fortunately, this decentralization is fairly simple, and in fact is a part of some governmental science promotion programs. In England, for example, a great deal of the science promotion was done through the University Grants Committee that simply gave grants to various universities to use in any way they saw fit. This involved the centralized provision of a subsidy and the decentralized determination of what should be subsidized. There seems to be evidence that on an informal level this English institution is now becoming more centralized. It would appear that the individual universities are now beginning to feel subject to a certain amount of pressure to direct their research in ways that meet the general consensus. This may be an inevitable development, but it certainly is unfortunate.

[2] See Gordon Tullock, *The Organization of Inquiry* (Durham, N.C.: Duke University Press, 1962).

In the United States there are a number of highly centralized governmental institutions supporting research, such as the National Science Foundation and the National Institutes of Health, but there are also methods of subsidizing research that are highly decentralized. The most decentralized institutions of all, of course, are the provisions in the tax code that make it possible for most corporations to consider most of their research expenditures as current expenses rather than as investments. Since the corporate tax is a heavy one, this amounts to a large subsidy for corporate research activities. Furthermore, it is, of course, completely decentralized. Any corporation is free to perform research in any area it wishes. Note, however, that this particular system of subsidizing research on the whole is simply a way of strengthening the patent system, and it does not have much to do with the production of pure research. This, of course, is no objection.

There are, however, in the United States and indeed in many other countries, arrangements under which individuals may make gifts to institutions engaging in pure research and deduct the amount of these gifts from their income for tax purposes. This again is a highly decentralized governmental subsidy to pure research. There is no obvious reason to believe that it is an optimal subsidy in any sense, but it is difficult in this area to determine what an optimal subsidy would be. In this connection, it seems likely that scientific research in general is one of the most lightly taxed activities in almost all countries. Since scientific research receives the same government benefits as do other activities, and pays little in the way of taxes, in a sense it is rather heavily subsidized.

But are these subsidies enough to deal with the externalities involved in this particular type of public good?

Unfortunately, there is no way of telling. We have no method available for determining what is the optimal amount of research in society, and it is perfectly possible that we are engaging in much too much research. It is, in other words, perfectly possible that we are devoting more resources to providing information for the future than we really should. In my opinion this is not so; we are probably still underinvesting in research in certain areas, but this is a personal opinion and I have no convincing arguments to support it.

Most scientists are likely to feel that the statements in the last paragraph are not only wrong, but are foolish. Most scientists are absolutely convinced that research, and in particular the type of research they are involved in, should receive far more resources. Not long ago, for example, a committee of leading American scientists actually reached the formal conclusion in a report to the government that governmental policy should increase the resources invested in science at a rate of 15 per cent per year on a permanent basis. This recommendation instead of being ridiculed by the remainder of the scientific community was actually treated with great respect. It does, of course, indicate, in a way, that scientific research is necessary. How could a group of rational men seriously recommend that, in a nation in which the national income is growing at a rate of 3 to 5 per cent per year, the support for science be indefinitely increased at the rate of 15 per cent per year. The fact that many of them were extremely skilled mathematicians makes the research problem particularly difficult.

In most Western countries "science" is politically powerful and is able to obtain fairly large governmental appropriations for its support. In the United States there was a considerable period in which the appropriations for science grew by about 15 per cent per year. Naturally, as the total amount invested in science grew at this rate, it eventually became large enough so that it significantly competed with other uses of money, and the politicians began to crack down. At the moment, governmental participation in science is still a growing activity in the United States, but naturally not at the earlier rate of increase. Many other countries have had somewhat the same experience, and West Germany, which is currently rapidly expanding its commitment to science, will no doubt go through the same development in the near future.

A second problem that must be faced in attempting to deal with how heavy our commitment to science should be is the fact that a great deal of science is undertaken by individuals essentially for their own entertainment. This is particularly true of the very best scientists. Second, a very large part of science is undertaken on what may be called an "undirected management" system. A great many universities hire their faculty and then employ them in teaching for only part of their time. The faculty is expected to spend the rest of the time producing research, and this research is evaluated largely by counting the number of pages published. Once again, we have a subsidy with extreme decentralization. Since the present institutions for doing this are fairly large, it is by no means obvious that further subsidies are necessary.

In sum, then, scientific research produces an externality. In fact, it is almost possible to say that it produces a pure externality. Like other "public goods," the addition of one more consumer does not increase the cost. For pure research, at any event, the effects of the research are twofold: enjoyment on the part of the researcher and an increase in knowledge for everyone including the researcher. The second, surely the larger effect in those cases in which the research is worth doing, is a pure "public good." Thus, this is an area in which private benefit would be greatly different from public benefit and subsidization would seem to be called for. The countervailing features are simply that this is also an area in which a decentralized control of funds is highly desirable. The two can be mated by arranging for a centralized subsidy that is administered in a highly decentralized way. It is possible that tax rebates are the most efficient way of meeting these two requirements, but we need a great deal of empirical research before we can say for certain what method of subsidy should be used.

If it is difficult to determine the optimal way of administering a subsidy in this area, the difficulty in determining the optimal size of the subsidy is even greater. I know of no even moderately respectable method of computation. The normal political method is simply to express a strong preference for some particular amount of subsidy for some particular collection of scientific projects. That this is a most unscientific procedure is obvious. What is not obvious is what we should put in its place. Here it would seem that we do need a good deal of research. It would not appear impossible to compute the return on research funds invested in the past. If we have such a rate of return figure, then we could combine this figure with some idea of the rate at which returns decline on investments in this area and obtain a desirable amount of research for the future. This, then, could be used to determine the appropriate level of subsidy.

Unfortunately, scientists in general are extremely vigorous in claiming great value for science and are extremely reluctant to let anyone measure it. The extreme criticism that "Operation Hindsight" roused in the scientific community is an example of this phenomenon. Nevertheless, although it is certainly true that scientists are pained by any effort to obtain measurement of the value of their output, sensible social policy requires that we create such measures. Unfortunately, in this area an individual scientist would probably be seriously penalized by his colleagues for undertaking research. Thus, the private cost of such research would be extremely high, and the social benefit would also be very high. It would seem that any program for stimulating scientific research should provide for the stimulation of scientific research on the value of scientific research.

It may seem to the reader that this chapter has been extremely indefinite. The statement is accurate, but the implied criticism is not just. Our knowledge in this area is poor, and it is difficult to improve it. We need further research into research. There are, however, certain things that are clear. One of these is that research is a generator of public good, and, hence, that the private market would probably produce less research than is desirable, from the standpoint of society as a whole. A second thing that is obvious is that the financial support for this activity should be highly decentralized. The problem is that there is no way of telling how large the subsidy should be. It is perfectly possible that the present subsidies are an order of magnitude too large or an order of magnitude too small. Thus we have an interesting situation in which we can prove very definitely that governmental activity is desirable, but we do not know whether this proof indicates that present government institutions should be expanded or contracted. Perhaps one of the readers of this book may be able to solve the problem.

# ( 13 )

# Speech and
# Information

The general subject of freedom of speech and restrictions upon it is surrounded by magic and ritual. It is apparently such a sacred subject that there has been little or no scientific discussion of it. If any of my readers feel bound by the taboo, I suggest that they bypass this chapter. Meanwhile, for those who will not be offended, and I hope there will at least be some, I should like to apply the concepts of externality in this area.

It is clear that speech may have great externalities. Let us suppose, for example, that I undertake a vigorous anti-Semitic propaganda campaign; surely, even though no Jew listens to me, some people are injured. Similarly, if I were to undertake a major campaign urging that Negroes be given greater opportunities than they now have and this campaign had any effect, a number of people who are not involved in my campaign would benefit (and some would be hurt). This subject is normally not mentioned in discussions of freedom of speech, but general public knowl-

233

edge of these externality effects is implicit in discussions of specific public utterances.

The April 27, 1968, *Economist* gave its lead article to an attack on remarks by Enoch Powell on the British race issue. The entire editorial is, in essence, a plea for certain people, mainly Powell, to remain silent on the grounds that their remarks will lend support to undesirable opinions. "For the Tories to continue this opposition to the bill in the cruder atmosphere of party meetings in the country would be disastrous. It would be bound to inflame the racial problem." [1] As another example, Raymond Aron, in his reply to General de Gaulle's remarks about Israel said:

I am not indifferent to the objections raised by some people, including even some of my friends. The only proper answer, they say, to such an insidious and evil thesis is silence. By taking notice of evil you aggravate it—you furnish arguments for your opponent—you will never strike the right note—you will be either too aggressive or too much on the defensive— you will only irritate both your non-Jewish fellow country- men and your "co-religionists." [2]

The campaign, vigorously in operation at the time at which I write, against violence on television and in movies is an- other example of efforts to reduce the externality generated by expression.

The injuries and benefits can result entirely from pri- vate action, but it is also possible to generate externalities by causing government action. Let us suppose that my pro- Negro campaign leads to the enactment of legislation. History indicates that the propagation of ideas sometimes leads to government activity. This could well cause gains

[1] *Economist*, April 27, 1968, p. 13.
[2] *Encounter*, June 1968, p. 7.

to certain people and injuries to other people who were not involved in the information campaign at all.[3]

A third externality that may be raised by "speech" and other "communication" is the direct offense or benefit from the communication itself. Let us say, for example, that I advertise some commodity. The people who see the advertisements may either gain or be injured by them. Furthermore, a great many of the people who see my advertisements, practically regardless of the way in which these advertisements are disseminated, will be people who are not likely to purchase whatever it is that I am advertising. Thus, the externality in this case is particularly pure. Let me give two examples. First, Chrysler has been recently running some advertisements of the Imperial that are illustrated by a picture I personally find extremely satisfying. It is very unlikely that I will ever buy an Imperial, but I clearly receive some aesthetic satisfaction from this advertisement. I think, by any definition that this should be regarded as an externality. Second, when I drive to work in the morning I can hardly avoid seeing a large billboard that has been rented by an art gallery. The gallery displays on the board an example of the type of art that it sells as well as its name and location, and I find this particular painting extremely offensive.[4]

To repeat what I said at the beginning of this chapter, most people do not think about these matters in a scientific way. Thus many people say that they believe in the total

[3] Perhaps the clearest case of this type of externality, though, would involve foreigners. Government action that arises from opinion within the country and affects foreigners is quite common.

[4] In order to avoid misunderstanding, I should explain that the picture is not in any sense pornographic. It is, in fact, a picture of a small girl who is fully clothed holding a flower. It is my artistic sensibilities that are offended, not my political or social conscience.

freedom of speech. I can usually convince such people very quickly that they do not. It normally, of course, requires my knowing something about their personal preferences and thus, producing some example of speech that they find particularly revolting, such as anti-Semitic propaganda, certain statements about Negroes, arguments against "academic freedom," and finally, for almost all academics, lengthy and carefully thought-out courses in their particular subject teaching material (or, as they would say, indoctrinating material) that is directly contrary to what they believe should be taught. The Department of Astronomy is not likely to turn its elementary course over to an enthusiastic "flat-earther."

Normally, having met someone who has stated he believes in total freedom of speech and presented him with whatever case I think is most likely to give him offense, I get a statement from him that freedom of speech does not mean completely unrestricted speech.[5] There may also be various technical efforts to "wiggle out" of the freedom of speech issue by such devices as maintaining that teachers who do not teach "correctly" are not competent. Nevertheless my experience indicates that almost nobody believes that speech and other forms of communication should be completely unrestricted.

There is, however, one area in which most democrats are opposed to more than the absolute minimum of restrictions on speech. This is the political area. It is generally believed by most people that it is undesirable to give the

---

[5] At this point a distinction is frequently made between "freedom" and "license." As far as I can see, this distinction is very simple: "Freedom" is something I approve of; "license" is something I do not approve of.

government the power to restrict political arguments. The reasons normally given for this restriction tend to be ritualistic and deal with higher values. There is, however, a fairly common down-to-earth explanation. We fear that the government, given the power to restrict political comment, will make use of this power to ensure its continuance in office, thus making it impossible for dangerous criticism of its own activity to be voiced. A recent example of this occurred in England in which the government made an effort, albeit an unsuccessful effort, to conceal a security scandal through uses of the security rules.

Note, however, that even at this level we normally do not feel that total lack of restriction on freedom of speech is desirable. As one obvious example, banning anti-Semitic or anti-Negro propaganda is frequently favored by people who are great enthusiasts for "free speech." They may go further. Much of the American press media, television in particular, has been badgered (partly by organized pressure groups and partly by administrative action) into presenting pro-Negro propaganda. Originally, this activity consisted mainly of attempts to introduce Negro characters into television in roles that they did not often play in actual life. This was normally urged by arguments rather similar to those urged for socialist realism.[6] That is, proponents said that the television should present Negroes in roles that they played in the real world. By this they meant, like Stalin, the desired reality, not the accidents of the current appearances. I have almost never run into anyone who objected to this particular infringement on freedom of speech. I might even say that enthusiasm for

[6] The Chinese, more realistically, refer to the same phenomenon as revolutionary romanticism.

freedom of speech in the abstract is strongly correlated with enthusiasm for badgering the television stations into carrying this type of propaganda.[7]

Clearly, in this case we have what is thought to be a desirable externality. Many people, including myself, believe that if we can present to the average American a picture of a society in which Negroes occasionally play leading roles and regularly play roles other than sanitation workers, it is likely that the average man will object less when he sees a Negro in real life in these roles. Thus, the difficulties faced by Negroes in improving themselves will be lessened. We are attempting to generate a positive externality by exerting pressure on certain people to communicate "information" that in many cases is literally false because we would like to have the world different from what it is.

Here, then, we have an effort to change public opinion by controlling speech and communication. In principle this is not different from the South African press rules that are also an effort to change public opinion in what is thought to be a desired direction. The fact that we approve of one and disapprove of the other indicates that we have a certain set of preferences. It does not indicate that there is a difference in kind between them or that both of them are not efforts to generate externalities.

To continue, however, we generally do object to the

[7] Many people seem to think that freedom of speech and freedom of communication do not apply to television and radio. It is, of course, true that the Constitutional provisions date from before 1800 and do not mention radio or television. It may well be that a court could reasonably say the prohibitions in the Constitution do not extend into this area. Here, however, we are not talking about the existing Constitution but what are desirable institutions. It is clear that the arguments for permitting newspapers freedom are, if anything, weaker than the arguments for permitting television freedom.

government's using its power to control speech in order to obtain superior access to the voters for itself. Our objection in this respect is normally limited by a feeling that some restriction should be placed on communication. I know no one, for example, who would argue that the Atomic Energy Commission should publish a handy little book on how to make hydrogen bombs. Furthermore, the restrictions on knowledge about bacteriological warfare and how to start epidemics are, as far as I know, fairly widely believed to be desirable. At a somewhat more controversial level, other types of secrets having to do with our foreign policy and our military posture are widely approved. We have, however, a real problem in that the government may use these rules to protect itself against criticism. All of the experience that we have concerning government behavior indicates that this is a very real danger that is extremely difficult to avoid. Thus, we have an area in which the existence of an externality would suggest restrictions on communication. On the other hand, we suspect that the agency that would impose these restrictions (the government) would characteristically cheat. It is a difficult problem of balancing one consideration against the other, and there is very little that can be said in a general way.

There is, however, one comment that can be made here: the problem is essentially a problem of democratic government, not of all governments. If we look at history, or for that matter, inspect the present world, we realize that democracy is a rather exceptional governmental form. The normal forms of government, despotisms of one sort or another, normally make use of a large number of restrictions on information. The reason that they are able to do this is, of course, that the despot or clique that runs the government does not consider rules that might perpetuate itself in office to be offensive. Thus, they are willing to reduce externalities in communication to a much greater level than in a democracy. In part, this reduction of externalities, of course, is simply an effort to keep government in power. In part, however, it is more. There is an effort to genuinely improve efficiency by reducing externalities. It is certainly true that the ability to keep military matters extremely secret is an efficiency characteristic that improves the operation of both the military machine and diplomacy. This is an economy that despotisms obtain and that a democracy cannot because the people do not trust their government and hence do not wish to give the government the power to reduce these particular externalities.[8]

Thus far, we have been discussing methods by which governments could somehow change public opinion or the communications that people receive in order to obtain external economies or impose external costs. It is quite possible for private persons to do the same thing, and in fact they do. A particularly pure case concerns *The Atlanta Times*. Atlanta is a southern city with, as one would anticipate in a southern city, a considerable number of vigorous segregationists in its white community. The newspapers in the city, all owned by the same organization, however, were "liberal." Seeing an opportunity, certain people formed a new paper called *The Atlanta Times* to represent the view of what was possibly a majority of the white population. The paper was extremely successful initially, but it was eventually driven into bankruptcy. This

---

[8] In both cases, the people do not trust their government. Probably they distrust it more in the case of despotism. The point is that popular distrust is irrelevant in the case of despotism.

bankruptcy came from the fact that the Negro community organized a boycott against anyone who advertised in *The Atlanta Times* and the other Atlanta papers appear to have (there is no proof of this) indicated that advertisers in *The Atlanta Times* would have difficulty getting good space in the other papers. This was clearly an effort by certain private citizens to change the existing flow of "information" in the community for their benefit. They were attempting (completely successfully) to eliminate an externality by private activity.

More generally, public relations is an effort to change the flow of information in society, as is the field of advertising. Both of these "arts" are used to affect political behavior as well as to affect private purchases. Thus, if I would like a tariff placed on a commodity that I manufacture, I might organize a campaign to change public opinion so that the government would enact such a tariff. This type of activity absorbs the talents of some of the best minds in society. Clearly, here we have a private effort to control externalities generated by information.

As a special case of communication externalities, I might tell Mr. Smith that Mr. Jones was a retired bank robber now living on the proceeds of previous robberies. This might exert an externality on Mr. Jones. In the Anglo-Saxon world, if the statement is not true, this particular type of externality is dealt with by the libel law. In much of the rest of the world, statements that might injure another person may be actionable, even if they are true. We are beginning to develop something like this in our law of privacy. The law of privacy is currently in a rather confused state, but it would appear that truthful statements about other persons that injure them may be actionable.

Here, again, we have an effort to reduce one particular type of private action in which communication of information is thought to create a negative externality.

As another example, urging someone to commit a crime is likely to cause a negative externality. Although the law on this point in most parts of the democratic world is highly confused, the reasons for this confusion, I think, are two historical facts. The first of these is that we only rarely have historical examples of people publicly urging the commission of crime. This is, in practice, rare behavior and therefore there is little legislation concerning it. The second reason for this restriction is also historical and has to do with the fact that during the latter part of the nineteenth century and the early part of the twentieth century a number of political organizations were formally in favor of revolution and assassination. They had enough general political support so that direct restriction of their activities was apparently impossible in democracies. They were, therefore, able to enact into the law some principles that left their propaganda mostly free from restriction. It should be noted in this connection that, although these political groups talked a great deal about revolution and assassination, the number of actual revolutions and assassinations was very small. Thus, it may well be that considering them as harmless was the proper approach.

Nevertheless, it is fairly clear that one could make externality arguments for prohibiting people from urging others to commit crimes against third persons. Whether these crimes be riots, revolutions, assassinations, or simply bank robberies would seem to make relatively little difference. The fact that this is a rare and unusual type of "speech," and that characteristically it does not lead to any positive action is probably the reason that few laws currently prevail in this area. In regard to external economy, indoctrinating people to obey the law, to refrain from murder, and to respect the Constitution are also externality-generating activities. One of the major activities in all educational systems is indoctrinating children with such precepts. Here we have another effort to reduce externalities by changing the information pattern.

Thus far we have been talking entirely about public methods of dealing with these problems. Private agencies may also contribute. Churches, for example, are privately supported agencies that indoctrinate people in moral precepts. Clearly, this is, in part, a way of providing privately subsidized propaganda in order to obtain positive externality. I doubt, however, that many churchgoers think about it in these terms.

Private action to prevent the urging of crimes is somewhat less common. We do, however, have occasional situations in which people urge boycotts against media engaged in this kind of activity. I do not know how common these are, or whether they are particularly successful. On the whole, private persons who are worried about the crime rate and who wish to change the information climate in order to reduce the crime rate are more likely to attempt to subsidize private propaganda against crimes than to try and prevent propaganda in favor of them probably because there is usually very little public propaganda in favor of crime. I do not know whether this absence of propaganda indicates the existence of strong social sanctions.

The last type of externality received from communication is the type that I mentioned in connection with the art gallery's advertisement in Houston. In the course of communicating with people I may either offend the person

I am attempting to communicate with by telling him something that he would rather not hear, or I may offend other people who "overhear." As a simple example, consider the journal *Eros,* which was eventually banned under the pornography laws, although the case has been in and out of the Supreme Court for a long period of time. I may say that the following arguments are not the ones that the Supreme Court accepted in deciding that pornography prosecution was a suitable way of dealing with the problem.

Suppose that someone is publishing a journal that most people would regard as being extremely pornographic. Let us suppose, further, that he wishes to increase its circulation, and for this purpose purchases a mailing list and mails advertising that includes pictures of nude men and women engaging in sexual acts. Some of the people on the mailing list surely would under no circumstances think of subscribing to such a journal. These people are accidentally but inevitably included in the mailing. The pornographer's objective in purchasing the mailing list would be to acquire people who would be likely customers. It is simply a technological fact of the direct mailing industry that all mailing lists contain some people who are not likely to be interested in the particular thing advertised. For these people, the receipt of the advertising flyer with its pictures that they find offensive and that tells them that a journal (to them offensive) of this sort exists, is a negative externality.

Let us suppose, however, that among the people to whom we are actually addressing our advertisement, those who might conceivably subscribe, there are some who are offended by our advertisement. This also is quite possible. Here, again, we have caused a negative externality. The people who are interested in subscribing and who are benefited by receiving this particular piece of propaganda are the recipients not of a positive externality but of at least a benefit. There presumably are some other persons who like the pictures in the prospectus but who decide not to subscribe. They would be receiving a positive externality. It will be seen that substantially any method of public communication raises this problem. There always will be some people who see a billboard, watch the President's State of the Union speech on television because they have no alternative, or receive a direct mailing that they open in order to find out what it is. This is an externality, and it is extremely difficult to see how it can be handled; particularly since positive externalities may also be generated by this same activity.

Here we seem to have an area in which regulation could improve well-being, but one must note the dangers of political regulation. One of the characteristics of present-day American politics is that the President can obtain coverage by all of the television networks for any political statement he wishes to make, subject only to the requirement that he allege that it is not political. Clearly, this is an example of the administration's making use of its power to control the information media for its own benefit. One would anticipate that if the Federal Communications Commission began controlling to any extent statements made about political matters in order to reduce the offense received by certain people, that they would use their power in favor of the establishment.

It would appear, however, that strictly local controls might be possible in this area. If local communities simply prohibited direct mail advertising of a certain type, it is highly probable that a great many of the negative externalities of direct mail advertising could be eliminated.[9] Furthermore, it is on the whole unlikely that these restrictions would have very much effect on total information flow. The local communities simply have too little power. Also, and not unimportantly, the local community government is normally not much concerned with the major political issues and hence would probably not be interested in changing public opinion in the nation as a whole. This is particularly true since many of the information media are of nationwide scope in any event. Needless to say, the degree of externality reduction that could be obtained by local regulation is small, but the fact that it is a small benefit does not mean that we should not consider it.

However, this proposal, like much that I have said in this chapter, will no doubt shock many traditionalists. In general, I have found during conversations that almost everyone begins by saying that they are in favor of complete freedom of speech. A brief discussion will almost uniformly produce a variety of areas in which they feel that speech should be restricted. This normally, however, does not embarrass them. They simply redefine freedom of speech in an appropriate manner. The discussion is normally carried on in terms of emotion and cloudy ethics. The scientific approach that I have attempted to use in this chapter may, therefore, upset a good many people. Since I recommended at the beginning of the chapter that people who might be shocked ignore it, I do not feel I need make any apologies.

[9] This would require a Constitutional amendment, but we are talking on the level of science, not law.

# ( 14 )

# Income
# Redistribution

Income redistribution is one of the most important activities of the modern state. For many people, this is both an observation of what states do and a normative judgment of what they should do. From this point of view it may seem odd that a discussion of income redistribution has been put off to the end of the book. The reason for this is not an effort to discriminate against this particular governmental activity, but the fact that it does raise unique issues. Although there are efficiency aspects and externalities of some importance in income redistribution, the basic problems are nevertheless radically different. It seems sensible, therefore, to discuss this rather special subject in a separate chapter rather than distributing it in little bits throughout the rest of the book.

The proponents of income redistribution are seldom clear as to exactly why they desire it. I think this is not because they are trying to conceal their motives but because they think that their reasons are so obvious that they require no discussion. In fact, however, the reasons for desiring redistribution of income are rather complicated. Furthermore, I think that many of the programs we see in the real world have been organized under the slogans implying one particular set of motives but are actually aimed at serving another set. For this reason, it seems sensible to begin a discussion of externalities by a discussion of the reasons why we might want income redistribution.

The standard explanation for income redistribution is a desire to help the poor and downtrodden.[1] A person who wishes to help the poor may feel that it would be desirable that the poor have things given to them that they now do not have. Here, however, we come to a problem of the source of the gifts. I could, for example, be interested in helping the poor and deal with this desire by making a gift from my own pocket. This would be a free market activity. There is no reason why I cannot do it on any scale that I wish and if things were that simple, we could leave this activity entirely to the private sector. There are, however, some very great inefficiencies in both private and public charity, and they are perhaps worse in private charity.[2] Furthermore, as we shall learn, there are externalities involved. These externalities do not mean that I cannot make a gift to the poor, but they do provide a sort of external economy in giving gifts to the poor, so that I might be willing to make larger gifts to the poor through some kind of collective mechanism than I would be willing to make through individual gifts.

Let us now, however, pause to note that I might wish

---

[1] Some "charitable" projects aim at helping people who are ill regardless of their income level. The probable reason for this is a feeling that a person who is in pain is in a "bad way" regardless of the luxury of the surroundings in which he suffers.

[2] See Gordon Tullock, "Information Without Profit," *Papers on Non-Market Decision Making*, 1 (1966): 141–159.

to have the poor helped but not wish to help them myself (at least not wish that they get the major part of their help from me). I might feel that someone else (in most cases, people who are wealthier than I) should help the poor. Now it will be noted that if I have the power, because I am a voter, or because I am in absolute control, to force some other person (let us say, Mr. A) to transfer income to a poor person, Mr. B, then probably I have the power to force him to transfer that money to me and so (in a sense) I am making a direct charitable contribution to Mr. B. There would be, of course, cases in which I could compel Mr. A to transfer the money to Mr. B, but not compel him to transfer it to me. If this is so, then I am not engaged in charitable activity. In most cases, however, if I am able to manipulate the government to provide private transfer from Mr. A to Mr. B, I would also be able to divert the transfer from Mr. B to myself. Hence, I am in fact being charitable when I see that money goes to Mr. B. In any event, I shall for the present regard these two activities as being essentially charitable. A direct transfer of money to someone who is other than the person or persons who arrange the transfer, we shall call charitable, whether the source of the money transferred is the person who arranges the transfer or someone else.

If the income redistribution plans that are such a major part of modern state activity largely transferred money to the very poor, we could reasonably explain them in terms of this charitable motive. In practice, however, we find that the bulk of the beneficiaries of redistribution of income are not poor people. Undeniably some income is redistributed away from the very wealthy, although surprisingly little given their voting weakness, and some income is redistributed to the very poor, but the bulk of the redistribution is a shifting of money among people in the middle income bracket. This naturally brings us to the second possible reason for favoring income redistribution. I might favor income redistribution because I anticipate that I will benefit from it. I am, let us say, a farmer and I feel, correctly, that I will be much poorer if I have to sell my products in an ordinary competitive market. I therefore join with a number of fellow farmers and get from the government a program that raises my income. Naturally, I do not argue for this program in terms of the increase in my income. I may urge that it is necessary for the national defense or that it helps the poor, and of course there may be some poor who are helped. My basic motive, however, is to help myself. Most income redistribution activities in the government sector are motivated by pressure groups with this kind of simple, straightforward objective.

It is fairly easy to demonstrate that if a given redistribution of income is directed primarily by the people who receive it and who are not thought suitable objects of charity by others, then there is a loss to society from the transfer. If there are no persons other than Mr. A or Mr. B who are interested in the transfer from Mr. A to Mr. B, which would be true if Mr. B is not markedly poorer than Mr. A, then there are no externalities of a favorable nature, that is, no people who gain from the transfer except Mr. B. There are, however, some significant negative externalities: First, there is the excess burden of the tax that is used to raise the money for the transfer; second, is the excess burden caused by the delivery of the subsidy to Mr. B; and third, and probably vastly larger than either of these, is the large investment of resources in political maneuvering that is necessary to carry out the transfer. Thus, it would appear that those transfers of income, so common in modern states, that shift money from people who are politically weak to people who are politically strong are economically inefficient and cause significant waste. Needless to say, this argument is not conclusive in those cases in which money is transferred from one person to another and a third person benefits from it because for some reason (normally because the recipient is poor) he feels that this improves the distribution of income in society.

Having clearly distinguished between two possible reasons for favoring the redistribution of income, a desire to make a charitable contribution, and a desire to gain money for myself, I am now forced to point out that these two motives have been inextricably entwined by a great many very well-meaning scholars. The position was most clearly stated by Anthony Downs.[3] If I now discuss primarily the arguments offered by Downs, it will be because he states a widely held view with great clarity. If I am interested in helping a poor person, this is charity on my part. But from the standpoint of the poor person, his interest in receiving the money is not charitable, but simply a desire to benefit himself. The Downs argument points this out as true and suggests that we design governments in such a way that the poor are able to use their selfish desire to get money from the rich in order to compel the rich to make income transfers that are desirable for charitable motives. Downs assumes that ordinary majority voting provides the right amount of redistribution, but there is no reason to believe

[3] *An Economic Analysis of Democracy* (New York: Harper & Row, Publishers, 1957).

251

that this is so. It could just as well be true that we should give the poor (let us say) two votes for every one given to wealthy persons, or vice versa.

Furthermore, there is the question of the size of the government unit in which the transfer is to be made. Rothenberg engaged in unconscious circular reasoning with respect to this problem.[4] He started with an existing historically determined governmental unit to obtain the "right amount of redistribution," and then used this amount to design optimal governmental units. However, any application of this line of reasoning is necessarily circular.

It is probable that one could design a voting system to provide any given transfer of money to the poor from the wealthy. There is no obvious reason, however, to believe that any existing voting system is optimal in this sense. If I feel that the poor should receive (let us say) 5 per cent of the national income and I feel confident that the people who would be making gifts will, in fact, give only 2 per cent, I can probably arrange a constitution that compels them to make 5 per cent gifts. It is, however, hard to see any argument for this except simply my desire to force them to do something they do not want to do. It seems simpler to avoid all problems of voting procedures and just set up a flat rule that they must give whatever I feel is the right amount instead of concealing the imposition of my preferences upon them under a voting rule.

Regardless of these rules, what we actually observe in democracy is that majority voting does not redistribute much money to the poor and does redistribute a great deal

---

[4] "Decentralization, Externalities, Equity, and Inter-Government Relations," presented as a paper at the Conference of Universities-National Bureau of Economic Research, Committee of Production and Distribution of Public Products (April 26–27, 1968). To be published in a *Proceedings* of this conference.

of money to people who are by no means poor. This last activity, as we have noted, is almost a total social waste. It may seem perverse, after this discussion of what actually happens in a democracy, to confine oneself to discussing only that type of redistribution of income that actually benefits the poor, but that is the purpose of the remainder of this chapter. My point is simply that this is the only type of redistribution that can be justified by externalities. Redistribution from one group of middle class people to another is not a way of generating favorable externalities, although it will usually generate unfavorable externalities.

Turning then to the pure problem of charitable redistribution, we should remember that there is no reason why any individual who is concerned with the poor may not transfer money to the poor himself. There are, however, two reasons to believe that the transfer of funds we would obtain in this manner would be less than optimal. In this sense, note that we are discussing the optimum for the man who is making a transfer, not the optimum for the poor person who is receiving the money. Clearly, any amount received will be gratefully accepted.[5] Thus, in determining an optimum, we must leave aside the preferences of the recipients. The poor person is simply a special example of those persons who wish transfers to themselves, and there is no reason why we should regard his desires as having any greater weight in designing the system than those of anyone else. The reason we help the poor is not that they wish to be helped, for, after all, I would like to be helped, but that other people wish to help them.

The externalities concerned with helping the poor are essentially twofold. In the first place, if I am made un-

---

[5] Anyone doubting this may experiment by sending the author a check.

happy by a man starving in front of my door, and I give him some bread so that he does not die, this act not only benefits me but it also benefits anyone else in the vicinity who is unhappy because of the starvation of this individual. Thus, I have created a positive externality for other persons and as is generally true, this situation would lead to an underinvestment in helping that starving man. This is a fairly simple example of a consumption externality, and it is a situation in which my consumption of something benefits other people as well, and hence the social optimum would call for a subsidy.

The second type of externality is rather more special and as far as I know is found nowhere except in the single example of charity.[6] Briefly, let us suppose that I am contemplating giving money to a poor man. I would continue making gifts to him until the value to me of one dollar transferred to him (that is, an improvement in his well-being by one dollar) is exactly equivalent to the one dollar cost to me. Suppose, however, that I enter into an agreement with someone else and we jointly give him the money. Under these circumstances, the cost to me of improving the poor man's well-being by one dollar is only fifty cents. Hence, I would extend charitable gifts to him until the benefit to me of his receiving one dollar equals the cost of fifty cents to me. Here we have a modifying feature. Presumably I have some interest in the well-being

---

[6] For a detailed technical explanation, see my comment on Marglin's "The Social Rate of Discount and the Optimal Rate of Investment: Comment," *The Quarterly Journal of Economics*, 78 (May 1964): 331–336. It may seem bizarre to cite a comment on another article as a primary source, particularly since my comment in this case is not original, but I think that this comment is clearer than anything else in the literature. Vickrey, who actually first thought of the idea treated it in an extremely brief, even cryptic manner.

of my cogiver and hence would take into account that he is also worse off by fifty cents, but my concern for him would be in general much smaller than my concern for the loss of a second fifty cents of my own. This is clearly a production externality. Note that this second type of externality in giving has two rather conspicuous characteristics: first, as the group engaged in making gifts grows larger, the effect on each member of the group falls off quite rapidly. In general, there is no great gain in increasing group size above a rather low maximum. A second point to be noted is that it assumes that the givers in a community all have exactly the same objectives. If I would like to make a gift to Mr. A, but the only agreement I can arrange with someone else is to jointly make a gift to Mr. B, I may indeed choose to make a larger gift to Mr. B than I would originally have given to Mr. A, but I will not be as well off as if I could have obtained the same agreement for the aid of Mr. A.

But, having established the existence of an externality in charitable gifts, when we turn to deciding on the optimum size of the unit to make the gift, we find ourselves almost immediately in serious difficulties. It would seem per se that the average individual might have either one of two types of preferences with respect to poverty. First, he might simply be interested in helping the poor defined in terms of income. This would mean that the geographical location of a poor person would not be of any great interest to him and he would make contributions entirely to an international charity that provided funds for the poor in low income areas. Since most of the people in the world who are really poor live outside the Western countries, and since most of the people who make large charitable gifts live in the Western countries, one would anticipate that charity would very largely be a process of transferring funds from the Western countries to the Eastern and African countries. Needless to say, this is not what we observe. There are some transfers by governmental means from the wealthy Western countries to the backward parts of the world, but these transfers are trivial compared to the transfers within the Western countries themselves.

Even if we confine ourselves to that part of the transfer of income within the Western countries that actually goes to the poor, a rather small part, it is still true that this transfer is much larger than the transfer to the poor of other countries. This is particularly true since most of the foreign aid programs are not aimed at helping the poorest people in the foreign countries. Thus, helping the poorest people is clearly not what modern democracies do.

The second possibility would seem to be that concern for the poor would vary inversely as the distance of the poor from the giver. The point of this particular preference pattern would be largely that I am distressed by the sight of the poor or by their near presence, and that the poor who live far away disturb me very little or not at all. Under these circumstances, one would anticipate that we would find charity lessening as we move away from individuals who are well off. If this latter pattern of preferences existed among charitable people, one could very readily specify an appropriate system of charitable disposition. One would anticipate the participation of local governments in considerable charity for people in their immediate vicinity; a larger level (say equivalent to the United States) engaging in a lower level of charity for everyone in their state; and finally a large government (let us say national) engaging in very low level charity for all the people in the country. We would anticipate that there would be more charity in the first category than in the second, or in the second than in the third. This would occur because each voter was more interested in charity for people close to him than in charity for people who were at intermediate or great distances from him. Once again, this is not what we observe.

It may be, however, that the present institutions represent not a true expression of people's preferences but a rather accidental survival from the 1930's. During the Great Depression, expenditures of federal funds were, to all intents and purposes, free since they contributed to recovery. Expenditures of local funds, however, did not have this fortunate effect, since the local governments could not print money. Under the circumstances, a transfer of many functions to the central government was sensible and relief (apparently a temporary but large expenditure) particularly so. It may be that the present organization of our relief, then, does not represent the shape of individual desires with respect to charity but is simply a hangover from this period. But this is only a possibility. What we need here is more research as to who people, in fact, do want to help. From this research we will be able to determine what the optimal unit for income redistribution is.

This chapter has been rather inconclusive. Charity may have externalities and hence may be a suitable area for governmental activity. We have been unable, however, to determine exactly what the government unit that is engaged in should be because it is impossible for us to tell much about the shape of individual preferences with respect to charity. This inconclusiveness is not a theoretical but an empirical defect. We need further information about people's desires with respect to charity before we can make any definite decision.

# 15

# Envoi

In a sense, the second part of this volume has been a routine exercise. The same standard approach has been applied to a large number of problems. In each case, we have examined the advantages or disadvantages that may be obtained by internalizing externalities. In each case, we have contrasted these advantages or disadvantages with the advantages or disadvantages involved in shifting from individual choice to group choice. This operation, which we have carried out in largely theoretical terms, can give an ideal solution for each activity. We can determine whether it would be best to leave it to the individual, whether it should be dealt with by a low level group such as a local neighborhood association, or whether it should be dealt with by a larger unit such as a nation or even a world government.

It must be emphasized, however, that the theoretical conditions that we have developed are just that. In almost every case, we need more empirical information to calculate the optimal outcome. As the reader has, no doubt, noticed, I have not been reluctant to express my own opinion on these matters. I think that my opinion is worthy of *some* respect, but what we need is not the opinion of a person who has thought a good deal about the problem, but serious empirical research in order to obtain the necessary data. In some cases this collection of data will require the discovery of new techniques, but in many cases, it involves perspiration rather than inspiration.

Traditionally, the decision between governmental provision of some good or service and private provision of the good or service has turned on rather irrational considerations. This is even more so if we consider a decision whether a given service should be produced by a local government unit or by a central government unit. We now have the necessary theory for making a genuinely scientific decision on this problem. It is always difficult to replace social tradition by science, but we should try. This book is intended as a step toward this goal. It is my hope that the readers of this final chapter will regard it not as an end but as a beginning.

# Index

## Index

N